Kingdom Horizon

Eight Reasons Why Earth's Greatest Days are Unfolding

by Robert Fraser

Kingdom Horizon: Eight Reasons Why Earth's Greatest Days are Unfolding

International Standard Book Number: 978-0-9753905-7-3

Published by:

New Grid Books
www.newgridbooks.com.

Edited by Dean Briggs

Cover Design: Srdjan Hadzic

Dedicated to Savannah

"Now I stroll at leisure with God
in the sunlit fields of life."
Psalm 56:13 (The Message)

You have bright future

Special thanks to:

Bob Hartley for your friendship and for starting me on this journey long ago.

Geoff Coventry, Mick Murray and Steve Magnuson for your invaluable input to this book.

Table of Contents

Table of Figures

Introduction

Sad to say, but hope has seen better days.

Confidence in the future is increasingly scarce. In developed countries, less than a third of people feel their children will be better off than they are.

Surprisingly, emerging countries are much more hopeful; more than half expect a better future. In communist Vietnam, 91% of people think things are improving.

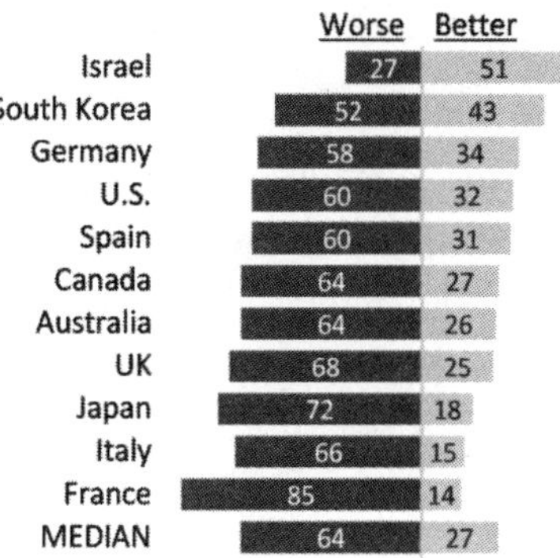

Figure 1 Optimism in Developed Countries

"Will Children Growing Up Today be Better Off or Worse Off?"

	Worse	Better
Vietnam	7	91
China	5	88
Nigeria	11	84
India	18	74
Chile	16	67
Peru	21	65
Brazil	35	61
Agentina	34	55
Indonesia	18	51
Pakistan	22	51
Philippines	26	51
Russia	19	48
Ukraine	19	48
South Africa	33	47
Mexico	43	41
Turkey	52	40
Venezuela	48	36
Poland	53	34
Jordan	37	32
Malaysia	49	30
Lebanon	47	24
MEDIAN	26	51

Source: Pew Research Center Values Survey, 2015

Figure 2 Optimism in Emerging Countries

Is the future really brighter in Vietnam, China or Nigeria than in America or Europe? Not likely! It shows the mindset more than the reality. In western society today, *declinism*—the belief that the world is getting worse—is rampant. And in Christian culture it is predominant. Pessimism, worry, fear and despair seem to be the very air we breathe.

My outlook was really no different. I gave my life to Christ in 1980 and I have since been a part of many different churches and church movements with wide-ranging emphases and vastly diverging views on eschatology. But throughout, there was a general presumption was that things were bad, getting worse, and about to get really ugly. I never really questioned this perspective myself, as it seemed obvious. I bought into it, and in my own limited sphere, propagated it as well.

Things began to shift for me several years ago. My world seemed full of people making poor life decisions due to short-term thinking and fear of the future. In many Christian circles it is not uncommon to see young people foregoing marriage or having children, not pursuing college degrees, not developing their careers, and not starting businesses; I've seen parents neglect their children's education, all for fear of the future. I've had friends prematurely sell prospering businesses, and I've watched others fail in business due to short-term thinking driven by fear of the future; and many of my friends have lost millions on doomsday investing.

Though I encouraged the opposite, this was the obvious fruit of pessimistic paradigms of the future. As a student of history, economics, scripture and science, I decided to put my paradigms to the test—setting aside my presuppositions and taking a fresh look at plain, unfiltered scripture and hard historical data to see where they would lead me. I was blown away by what my research uncovered. Thus began this book.

- I traced the roots of Christian pessimism and dread and discovered how it contrasted with the hope of early believers. It became Chapter 1.
- I am a professional big-data analyst and a confessed data nerd! I dug up every piece of data I could find on how the earth has changed since Jesus walked it—better or worse? I was unprepared for what I found. The story needed to be told, and so it shall be, in Chapter 2.
- I looked at what does the Bible really says about the future of the Kingdom of God. Barely understood today, yet scripture paints a clear and compelling picture (Chapter 3).
- My bookshelf is piled high with thirty years of doomsday books, and I knew their track record was atrocious. So I researched some of the major doomsday fears—past and present—and compared them to reality. Chapter 4 was born.

- The future of planet earth is another area Christians get stumped on. Destroyed by fire? Or Jesus reigning? Hint: We will find abundant reason for long-term thinking! Fasten your seatbelt for Chapter 5.
- In the best-selling book *The Harbinger*, author Jonathan Cahn laid out his case for judgment on America, and a chorus of eminent Christian leaders since have echoed similar sentiments. I have heard of only one arguing for mercy. I love my nation, and it seemed a bit overdone to me, and the logic flawed. So I did more research to see if there was any reason to hope for America. So begat Chapter 6.
- In Chapter 7 I take a fresh look at one of the main sources of fear today: Matthew 24; and in Chapter 8, I look at reasons why time is on our side.
- Finally, I wanted to know *why* exactly the early Christians were so excited about the return of Jesus. What did they know that we don't know? It was a bible study I will never forget, day after day of astonishment and joy as the lights slowly went on in my understanding. Wow! I hope Chapter 9 does for you what it did for me.

The single goal of this work is to show the abundant reason we have for hoping in the future—and in the process debunk the prevailing negative perspective that is so widely accepted you probably don't even realize how much its fundamental assumptions and subtle emotional chords govern you.

Concerning hope for the future, I will show that:

1. The facts agree

2. History agrees
3. The Bible agrees

My Own Journey

On this journey, I don't want to live and die outside the greater promise of God. I want to move in greater faith than ever before. I'm a Bible-believing literalist, a confessing, conservative Evangelical, committed to the infallibility of scripture. I deeply love the church and don't have an axe to grind. Yet I see the real and damaging fallout from fear-based paradigms. I know the language and central premises by heart, because I taught them to others. I know how a few faulty paradigms have turned our wildly good news into bad news, and diverted the precious disciples of Jesus from taking their Promised Land to putting their destiny in "park" while awaiting doom and decline.

I want to be absolutely clear that I'm not pointing a finger at any person or teacher individually, but rather an overall culture of pessimism and dread that is common today. In Chapter One, I will necessarily take on one key individual, a man named John Nelson Darby, mainly because most of the false paradigms can be traced back to him, so the association is unavoidable. Otherwise, I want to stay in the realm of ideas and consequences, scripture and fact.

Which leads me straight to my own prediction regarding *you.*

Dear Reader...

Here is my hopeful, prayerful prediction for your encounter with this book.

1. By the end of the first three chapters, I predict you will start to feel strangely liberated. At the beginning, it may feel like grinding gears as new ideas engage the old presuppositions. That's good!
2. By the middle, you might start to feel a new hope dawning, a fresh breeze in your soul, and freedom to live and breathe and dream.
3. By the end, however, like leaping in a pool on a hot summer day, you will find yourself swimming in the deep end of a new and vigorous hopefulness.

Over and over scripture admonishes us to hope, believe, trust, risk, dare, overcome and triumph. Will you join me on that journey? If so, this is where we start: let's put on some hope.

CHAPTER 1

Reason #1

THERE IS HOPE FOR THE FUTURE

Fact:
"Looking for the blessed hope and glorious appearing of our great God and Savior Jesus Christ"
Titus 2:13, NKJV

It seems to be a widely held notion today that chaos is destined to consume the planet—and Christians are often its chief proponents. Our bookshelves, airwaves, newspapers, podcasts and pulpits are filled with bad news, all supporting the obvious conclusion: our future is dim indeed.

You may be as surprised as I was to learn just how big the doom business is. For decades, apocalyptic movies have been some of the most reliable hits at the box office. I recently added up the number of titles. Do you realize that in the last fifty or so years,

Hollywood has given us *230 apocalyptic movies,* which I define as films with some form of apocalypse as their major theme?

The doom business is *big* business. Consider the enormous windfall proffered by the purveyors of Christian apocalyptic literature, as incontrovertibly evidenced by the New York Times Best-seller List. The *Left Behind* series alone has sold a mind-boggling 65 million copies, which isn't a new phenomenon. In the 1970s, a famous little book by Hal Lindsey called, *The Late, Great Planet Earth* became *the highest selling non-fiction book of the entire decade*, not just in religious titles, but *all* non-fiction, both secular and religious. It deeply impacted a generation, launching countless waves of speculation and attention to global chaos as a Biblical predictor of the Lord's return.

Many predictions and prophets[1] have followed:

- Jerry Falwell predicted that in 2000 the Lord would pour out his judgment on the world.
- Tim LaHaye and Jerry Jenkins, writers of the *Left Behind* series, said that the Y2K Bug would trigger global economic crisis and the Antichrist would use it to rise to power. (In all fairness, they changed their minds, which means they're in good company!)
- In his 1990 book, *The New Millennium,* Pat Robertson suggested that April 29th, 2007 would be the day of the Earth's destruction.

---

[1] For example, in his work, *Observations upon the Prophecies of Daniel, and the Apocalypse of St. John,* no less a figure than the esteemed Isaac Newton predicted that Jesus would return in 2000. Jonathan Edwards said much the same, figuring the year 2000 would mark the beginning of the millennial reign of Christ.
(*en.wikipedia.org/wiki/list_of_dates_predicted_for_apocalyptic_events#cite_note-hs-20)*

- Many feared that the famous Mayan Apocalypse of December, 2012 would bring unprecedented upheaval to our planet.

The latest round concerned the notorious "Blood Moons" phenomena, which launched several books and much handwringing. Due to their particular timing and frequency during the years 2014-2015, these otherwise normal lunar cycles have somehow become harbingers foretelling terrible things for our future. *Blood Moons* author Mark Blitz, expected wars in Israel, economic collapse and the collapse of the dollar[2] (I address these in Chapter 4). A quick search for September 2015 blood-moons showed expectations of the earth's destruction by asteroid impact[3], Isaac Newton's end of the world prophecy, a particle collision at CERN's new hadron collider that would open up a wormhole or spiritual portal, and a meeting between the Pope and President Obama that could usher in the new world order.[4]

This is hardly a complete list, but it doesn't need to be to make the point.

Doomsday Beliefs Are Widespread

Back in 1999, *Newsweek* shared some mind-blowing research. They surveyed a bunch of adults in the United States across a spectrum of beliefs, Christian and otherwise, and this is what they found. They asked the question, "Do you believe the world will end with the Battle of Armageddon as described in the Book of

[2]www.wnd.com/2015/09/why-this-coming-blood-moon-is-important-to-watch/
[3]www.express.co.uk/news/science/592987/End-of-the-world-asteroid-Blood-Moon-September-apocalypse-armageddon-comet-meteor
[4]www.truthlamp.com/apocalypse-september-23-2015/

Revelation?" An incredible 40% of Americans answered yes![5] Not 40% of Christians, mind you, but 40% of *all Americans*. In our highly secularized society, that's an amazing statistic. Among Evangelical Christians, that figure jumped to 71%!

Furthermore, of those that believe Armageddon is going to happen, 47% believed that the Antichrist was already alive on Earth (in 1999), while another 45% believed Jesus Christ would return during their lifetime. The point of these statistics is the pervasiveness of what is called "imminence" in popular theological language. In the same 1999 Newsweek poll, 15% of responders, representing over 50 million American adults, believed that Jesus would return as early as the year 2000 (within a year of the poll)!

40% of all Americans "believe the world will end with the Battle of Armageddon as described in the Book of Revelation."

Amongst those people who believed Jesus would soon return, expectations for disaster were even higher:

- 83% said His second coming will be preceded by natural disasters
- 66% by epidemics
- 62% by mayhem

[5] "Prophecy: What the Bible Says About the End of the World," Newsweek, 1999-NOV-1, as reported in AANEWS for 1999-OCT-25.

Bottom line, doomsday belief is prevalent in the earth, and amongst Christians, it is predominant. The return of Jesus is viewed as a very negative and imminent event. At this stage, rather than arguing about theology or the number or degree of challenging times that may lie ahead of us, I simply want to recognize that, in the popular, collective mind, the future adds up to being very dark and troubled. We might know it's supposed to be good in our head, but our hearts and emotions carry a clear measure of dread. Ninety-five percent told *Newsweek* they felt that they must "get right with the Lord" as a result. Clearly, this is the positive side of these teachings.

A pervasive pessimism has been woven into the fabric of our faith. It seems a belief in doom has become synonymous with Christianity. But even if the gravest of challenges await us, *is this really to be our perspective*? Whatever happened to the "good news?" When did our news turn bad? Have we become the undertakers of society, morbidly awaiting the next big act of death and destruction? My friends, I tell you, *this is not who we are to be*. When Proverbs 31:25 describes the virtuous wife as someone who "smiles at the future," it is actually describing the ultimate virtuous wife, the Bride of Christ, the church. She *smiles* at the future. She is unafraid. Confident. Bold. Industrious.

A belief in doom has become synonymous with Christianity

Where Did This Come From?

Historically, the church has by-and-large held a positive view of the future. The shift in perspective began about 200 years ago, as the byproduct of the rise of a new teaching called Dispensationalism. It was popularized by British theologian, John Nelson Darby, who lived from 1800-1882. Darby was a great theologian and a very influential preacher and reformer in the Church.

Darby taught that the End-Times would begin with the Rapture, and then the Antichrist would come, along with the mark of the Beast and the Battle of Armageddon, followed by the return of Christ. The Rapture would be a surprise that would kick off the Final Act. Darby's most powerful idea was that *we could tell we were getting close by monitoring natural disasters and social decay*. Though much of his framework was Biblical—its popularity, in fact, can be attributed to its literal, chronological comprehensibility—it produced powerful and unintended consequences of pessimism and dread.

Darby's most powerful idea was that we could tell we were getting close by monitoring natural disasters and social decay

Dispensationalism's ascent can be traced to the wildly popular Scofield Bible, which filled its pages with Darby's teaching and methodology. Conservative pastors began preaching Dispensationalism, which then exploded into mainstream thought in more recent times via Lindsey's mega-influential, *The Late Great Planet Earth.* A huge influx of Jesus Movement disciples began to fixate on charts and signs. The *Left Behind* series was basically *The Late, Great Planet Earth* told in a series of novels. By then, Dispensationalism had become the de-facto interpretation of future events, fostering a rigidity of thought and passion for its central premise that left little room for other ideas. Whether you know it or not, if you are an Evangelical, chances are that you have largely accepted the terms and conditions of Dispensationalism *carte blanche.* Darby's system is like a drug prescription with no dosage guidance. The balancing perspective of other scriptures has largely been neglected, or lost altogether.

> Dangerous technological advances during the Age of Steam and the Age of Electricity—such as the telegraph and telephone!—all indicated the end was near

The above gives a very brief overview of the theological development. Dispensationalism is the Idea. Pessimism and dread are the consequences. Here's how it went down in psychological and sociological terms within the church. In the wake of Darby's Dispensationalism, conservative Christians in the 1800s and 1900s began to infer Biblical meaning from historical events (whether it was there or not) and thereby draw all kinds of foreboding conclusions from many different moral, technological, and geopolitical trends. This was not accidental. It is in the DNA of prophetic belief to seek out circumstances that confirm your doomsday timeline.

Thus, rumors of wars and other societal ills, along with certain dangerous technological advances during the Age of Steam and the Age of Electricity—such as the telegraph and telephone!—all indicated the end was near.[6] While that may seem laughable now, this trend never abated, it only *updated.* Headlines have changed, but the skewed paradigm remains. So whenever one prediction fails, we blithely scratch out the wrong answer and fill in a new one, never once questioning the underlying paradigm driving our need to find prophetic doom in current events.

Let me give you a few examples:

1. In 1935, President Franklin Delano Roosevelt's introduces the Social Security Act. Christians, looking for the definitive "sign of the times," feared FDR's actions were forcing the "mark of the beast" on society. After all, everyone *was assigned a number.*[7]
2. Eighty years later, the social security system has not led to societal control, so the target moved. Perhaps we should be afraid of credit cards?
3. New update. It's biochips[8]...humans are being marked...
4. No, wait. It's the *internet.* "Www" is 666[9]. The internet is everywhere, business depends on it, and you can't escape. The internet is the Beast of the Book of Revelation.

---

[6] www.pbs.org/wgbh/pages/frontline/shows/apocalypse/explanation/amprophesy.html#darby
[7] www.papergreat.com/2014/01/vintage-foreboding-religious-tract-mark.html
[8] www.av1611.org/666/biochip.html

My larger point is not to casually dismiss a legitimate concern for certain social or technological trends, but to recognize the never-ending quest for signs. We desperately want to confirm our mile-marker in history. While the heart may be sincere, the methodology is flawed. The latest version of the fill-in-the-blank fear is the use of RFID on credit cards. Where does it stop? When do we finally say, "Enough!"?

Aren't We Being Hard On Darby?

I told you I had to tackle Darby head on, but maybe you feel I'm being unfair to Darby. Maybe all this is just my opinion. Is Darby really to blame? Well, according to a staunch supporter like Tim LaHaye, author of the *Left Behind* book series,

> "Darby figures to be a central figure in any study of the pre-tribulation Rapture. There is little question that he, more than any other man, popularized this view in both the United States and Britain."[10]

So let's let Darby speak for himself:

> "Instead of permitting ourselves to hope for continued progress of good, we must expect a progress of evil; and that the hope of the earth being filled with the knowledge of the Lord before the exercise of His judgment (i.e. the Second Coming) is delusive."[11]

---

[9] www.av1611.org/666/www_666.html

[10] Time LaHaye, *Rapture Under Attack*, Multnomah Press 1998

[11] Speech given in Geneva, 1840, in William Kelly, ed., *The Collected Writings of J.N.Darby*, Prophetic no. 1, vol. 1 (Kingston-on-Thames: Stow Hill Bible and Tract Depot, undated), 471, 486)

In other words, *we are deluded if we think there is any hope for the earth's future!* Earth is the Titanic, and it is sinking. By and large, Evangelicals have packed their bags and are awaiting the next lifeboat off the sinking ship. But what if the earth is not the Titanic at all? What if it actually has a great future? Then the only "left behind" are doomsday Christians who have abandoned their role in the greater plan of God in our rapidly advancing world.

My Titanic example may seem melodramatic or inflammatory, but in reality, it's a fair picture of the doomsday crowd today.

Producing Despair

An even deeper problem with this mindset is that it also governs our expectations. If you've heard of trickle-down economics, Darby's eschatology is like trickle-down despair. We unwittingly nurse our kids on the Biblical prophecies and fear. Some even ask, why have children at all?

My own child was one of them.

After my son heard some teaching on the End-Times, he came to me privately and confided, "Dad, *I don't want to have children, because the Antichrist is just going to kill them.*" He was 100% serious. My alarm bells starting ringing, and it was at that point I knew something might be wrong with the Kool-Aid we were drinking. That conversation was the first step toward flipping my switch on my doomy paradigm. When our theology of the *end* destroys the most basic human drive—procreation—and the most fundamental governing command given to the human race at the *beginning*, "Be fruitful and multiply" (Gen 1:28)—something is very wrong indeed.

Particularly in America, where evangelical denominations have thrived, the attitudes of Darby's theological children are generally conditioned to find the worst in everything. Friends, hear me: we're so negative! This leads to a powerful psychological-spiritual phenomenon that few recognize: We're almost *incentivized* each time something bad happens, since Darby told us that every bit of bad news actually confirms the Lord's return!

Darby went on to predict the absolute corruption of the church: "Christendom has become completely corrupted, the dispensation of the Gentiles has been found unfaithful: can it be restored? No! Impossible."[12]

Impossible? *Really*? The problem with the predominance of this view is that, in a fallen world, one can find "signs" of moral decay anywhere and at every point in history. Thus, zero discernment is required or applied to the interpretation of events. Anything bad is a sign of the times, and since there is plenty of bad stuff, the "doomsday-is-near" mentality never lacks fuel.

Calamities Accelerating?

One of the centerpieces of Darbyism is that as we get closer to the return of Jesus we will see calamities and disasters increasing. Isn't this what the Bible says?

Not at all.

Most, of course, are thinking of Jesus' End-Times discourse in Matt. 24: "wars, rumors of wars, famines, pestilences, earth-

---

[12] ibid

quakes and persecutions" (v. 6-8). But nowhere does Jesus claim these things will *increase*, but simply that they will *exist* at the time. He simply said, "There will be" (v. 7). Cognitive psychologists call it "selective perception"—where our expectations and biases determine our interpretation. Open your Bible and read it for yourself. *It's simply not there.*

The other great fear is the negative events in the book of Revelation. But they are all packed in tight sequence in the final few years of history—the period of the Antichrist. *There is no gradual increase over time.*

History confirms this as well. We find deaths per-capita from conflict *(Figure 14 Global Deaths in Conflict, p. 194*) and epidemics (see *Figure 24 Death from Epidemics, p. 199*) both dropping dramatically over the centuries. Though the number of people affected by disasters is up (see *Figure 8 Natural and Technological Disasters, p. 43*), it is only over the last 100 years. And even if it were, it doesn't change the fact that the Bible doesn't require such an increase.

Darby was wrong.

<u>Increasing Darkness.</u> Surely I can't dispute this one right? Everyone knows darkness is increasing…!

Is it?

We are certainly seeing evil advance on many fronts in many places. But taking a step back and looking across centuries instead of decades—has darkness really increased since the days of Nero and Caligula? Or the Viking Age? Or the Dark Ages? Or the times of the Black Death when a third of population of the planet died?

Or the times of Genghis Khan, when 11% of the globe's inhabitants were slaughtered? I am not so sure.

But doesn't the Bible predict increasing darkness? Well, the Bible predicts increasing light (I cover this in Chapter 3); and it also predicts the destruction of evil at the end, but doesn't say much about the growth or decline of evil between now and then. Jesus did say the gates of hell will not prevail against an advancing church (Matt. 16:18). And in the Parable of the Wheat and the Tares (Matt 13:24-30), God's crop of wheat grows and matures, as does the enemy's crop of weeds. But that does not necessarily imply increase.[13]

Darby may be wrong.

Decreasing Light. Sorry Darby, but scriptural support and historical evidence is overwhelming: *light is on the move*. If this is a crazy new thought to you, please bear with me for now—and make sure your seat belt is fastened for Chapters 2 and 3!

Darby was *dead wrong*.

A compromised, defeated Church. What about Darby's view of the Church as becoming completely corrupted and defeated? Again, there is simply zero support for this view, either scripturally or historically.[14]

---

[13] As in other passages, we may have wrongly equated *maturity* with *increase*. This is not necessarily the case. Maturity relates more to both quality and time than influence or proliferation. But even if an increase of evil is within view of this parable, this maturation is not in any way described in excess of the maturing increase of good. In fact, one does not completely dominate the other. More positively stated, if the tares were winning, they would completely choke out the wheat, right? It is the nature of weeds, as revealed in the Parable of the Sower (Matt. 13:1-23), to choke out the good seed. In the Parable of the Wheat and Tares, however, the wheat is revealed as healthy, prospering and thriving, albeit infested with a counterfeit, competing crop.

[14] Darby supported his view with a number of verses, 1 Tim. 4:1, 2 Tim 3:1-5, 1 Peter 4:17, 2 Peter 2:1-3, Jude 12-19, 2 Thes 2:3-12. While these verses point to various apostasies, they are not absolute or universal. Darby focuses entirely on the challenges facing the End-Times church but ignores that the Bride emerges "bright and pure" in the midst of them.

The church will become so strong and beautiful that by the end of the story, she is "without spot or wrinkle" (Eph. 5:27) and has "clothed herself with fine linen, bright and pure" which are her many "righteous deeds." (Rev. 19:8, ESV). While many dispensationalists embrace aspects of this truth, they miss the obvious consequence, that a church operating in "the measure of the stature of the fullness of Christ" (Eph. 4:13) *cannot but completely and utterly transform the fabric of the entire planet.*

A church operating in "the measure of the stature of the fullness of Christ" cannot but completely and utterly transform the fabric of the entire planet

The verse, "Having a form of godliness but denying its power" (2 Timothy 3:5) has often been applied to those who deny the power gifts of the Holy Spirit. But the verse does not identify those "denying the power of *God*," but the "power of *godliness*"—it is doubting the effectual power of *virtue* and light to transform what it touches. This verse more accurately fits those who see darkness prevailing. They rightly see the gospel as the prevailing power of God, *yet simultaneously assert its impotence at the end of history. That* is denying the power of *godliness.*

The Church Changes Trajectory

The Protestant Reformation in began 1517 as a theological revolution that shattered the oppressive religious paradigm of the day, bringing a revelation of the personal God, grace, and individual liberty.[15] It unleashed a complete paradigm-change in society. Within a few years it snowballed, unleashing a wave of capitalism, new music and vibrant universities. Within a hundred years, it spawned the greatest era of change in history: the Age of Enlightenment and the Scientific Revolution. There were breakthroughs in every sphere of life: inventions, new understanding in human rights, politics and liberty, the scientific method, mathematics, economics, chemistry, physics, electricity, medicine and art. It was led by men like Francis Bacon, René Descartes, Cesare Beccaria, Isaac Newton, Thomas Hobbes, John Locke, Jean-Jacque Rousseau, Adam Smith, Johannes Kepler, Robert Boyle, William Gilbert and thousands more.

Nearly all were Christians.[16]

They built nations[17]; they founded universities—106 of the first 108 universities in America were founded by Christians[18]; they engaged in science, politics and business. America was birthed, a risky, untested experiment in liberty, where they could put their grandest ideals into practice. Pastors, informed and articulate on the issues of the day, routinely published intelligent and reasoned sermons on politics and economics in newspapers.[19] To-

---

[15] www.encyclopedia.com/topic/Reformation.aspx

[16] Wilson and Reill note that, "In fact, very few enlightened intellectuals, even when they were vocal critics of Christianity, were true atheists. Rather, they were critics of orthodox belief." Wilson and Reill, *Encyclopedia of the Enlightenment* (2004). Atheism was much discussed but there were few proponents. Many enlightenment leaders were questioning the repressive, authoritarian church of their day. The Thirty-Years War between Catholics and Protestants, one of the most destructive conflicts in European history had just ended. And even as the Enlightenment was progressing in America and parts of Europe, the Spanish Inquisition was still zealously torturing and killing thousands in southern Europe and the New World to elicit confessions of unorthodoxy. Many intellectuals were rightly questioning the authority of the church and traditional church beliefs and teachings. However, that is very different from rejecting God altogether.

[17] www.heritage.org/research/lecture/2011/06/did-america-have-a-christian-founding

[18] Stephen McDowell, *Reforming America through Restoring America's Christian Education*, providencefoundation.com/?page_id=2530

[19] Ellis Sandoz, *Political Sermons of the American Founding Era*, oll.libertyfund.org/titles/816

gether, they became the greatest agents of positive change ever seen in history.

It was the *greatest inflection point in human history* since the days of Jesus. The trajectory of the planet shifted in every sphere, which is clearly visible in many of my charts. Static for 1500 years, suddenly economic growth exploded exponentially (see *Figure 4 World Population and GDP per Capita, p. 33*). In its wake followed breakthroughs in every measure of the quality of life, including health, education, and politics; notice the sudden improvements, all occurring at or near this time, in the mid-1700s, and continuing to the present day (see *Figure 23 Life Expectancy, p. 199*; *Figure 25 Literacy Rates, p. 200*).

The earth was on an accelerating trajectory, and Christians were at the helm.

The earth was their grand experiment, which they could mold and shape through new ideas and initiatives, discovering God's ways and devising how to express them on the planet.

Enter the teachings of John Nelson Darby in the mid-1800s. Without hope for the earth, or for the church, believers are taught to focus exclusively on evangelism, abandoning any idea of leading or influencing politics, education, science, media, the arts, economics, business, etc.

Today our most passionate young believers flock to missions programs like Campus Crusade for Christ and Youth with a Mission, which I love. But I wish as many also aimed to become eminent scientists, philosophers, professors, CEOs, politicians, reporters or artists. We have refrained from sending our sons and daughters into the world because of its darkness, even though *that is exactly what the Father did.*

"You are the light of the *world,*" Jesus said—not the light of the *church*; "You are the salt of the *earth,*" not the salt of *heaven.* Today we think of salt as a flavor, but in Jesus' day, before refrigeration, it was the only way to preserve food to keep it from spoiling. Fresh meat would rot within 24 hours, but meats cured with salt could last months. In naming the church as the salt of the earth, Jesus declared the church to be the *curative*, the *anti-rot* of the earth.

A church that is not focused on transforming the earth is a church that will become the doormat of society

That is, unless we lose our "saltiness"—our curative focus. Then only one thing is left:

> But if the salt loses its saltiness…it is then good for nothing but to be thrown out and <u>trampled underfoot by men</u>. Matt 5:13

Divine principle dictates that *a church that is not focused on transforming the earth is a church that will become the doormat of society.* Man-trampled. But it's not only is a principle, *it's a prophecy*, and it's being fulfilled in our day. The church points a finger at the world for being dark, but how can it be light without *us*? How can it be leavened unless we, the leaven, dive into the batch?

Today, the trajectory of the earth continues its exponential course as you will discover in the next chapter, but since the days of Darby, *without the church at the helm*. We have essentially abandoned our post on the bridge of our ship—earth!—and await our lifeboat to heaven, with our only purpose in the meantime to convince as many as possible to join us in line. Our Age of Enlightenment forefathers would be shocked.

The Fallout

Doom and despair paradigm has been toxic for the church:[20]

It produces a short term view. If the world is ending, why educate our children, build businesses, innovate, or influence our nations?

We stop building and investing in the future. Jesus spoke two similar parables *specifically* to address the delay in His second coming and instruct us what to do prior to His return: the Parable of the Talents (Matt. 25:14-30) and the Parable of the Minas (Luke 19:11-27). He told them, "*do business* until I come" (Luke 19:13). The message was clear: before the second coming, our *main focus is to live productive and fruitful lives*. But one was afraid and hid his talent. A pessimistic paradigm produces fear and causes us bury our talent, precisely what Jesus said *not* to do.

We don't influence the system for good. If we believe the earth is fated to destruction, and darkness is ordained to consume

[20] To give credit where credit is due, one clear positive of imminent Dispensationalism is the sense of urgency and readiness it tends to produce. Believers tend to live more attentively when they are alert to the Lord's imminent return. I want to retain the urgency and lose the fear. If premillennialists could root their eschatology in hope, I'm convinced we could become the most radical and urgent of all kingdom builders. I'll address this more in Chapter 8.

the planet, then we focus on our exodus from earth, rather than redemption of it.

We look for flaws in the system and rejoice when the system fails. Seeing the world as our enemy rather than our beloved mission, and its demise a sign of God's righteous judgment and imminent return, we can even find ourselves grimly satisfied by disasters and calamities that "prove us right." This is tragic beyond measure. It should never, ever be. We are to be the light of the world, not its undertakers.

We expect (and attract) the negative. Rather than pray for our nations, we pray against them. Because we believe demise is inevitable, and even warranted, we do nothing to stop it. We allow the enemy to plunder our house, though we have the power and authority to resist it. Our pessimism is actually negative faith – the things we fear come upon us. Rather than fighting evil, we prophesy on behalf of it.

We go broke. Many have sold successful businesses, and adopted flawed business strategies in trying to avoid economic calamities. Other have made nonsensical decisions such as investing in the Iraqi Dinar based on wild promises of wealth. Others have lost fortunes investing in gold and silver, or trying to profit from stock market crashes (even though the stock market goes up the majority of the time). While the world is busy producing wealth, a doomsday paradigm is a ticket to poverty.

We live under a perpetual cloud. One lady told me, "I feel like I am just waiting for the hammer to fall." Humans are not wired to live under despair. Studies show that a negative outlook even affects our health.[21] It sentences us to misery and hopelessness. It's no way to live.

Jesus had a very different vision for our role. We bear His presence within, like light. He called His people the light of the world, "a city set on a hill" (Matt. 5:14). He wanted us to engage the world. We must be proactive, not negligent or passive. Be constructive, not destructive. Don't *stop* building, start building. Don't *not* have babies, have babies! Don't look for a stock market crash, launch the next great enterprise.

The Early Church Was Not Afraid of the End

The first century church expected Jesus to return in their day. So you would expect them to be afraid, dismayed and despairing, right? Instead, they used words like "eagerness," "hope," and "joy" in describing His return:

> "Christ...will appear a second time...to bring to full salvation those who are [eagerly, constantly, and patiently] waiting for and expecting Him." (Heb. 9:27-28, AMP)
>
> "For we through the Spirit eagerly wait for the hope of righteousness by faith" (Gal. 5:5, NKJV)
>
> "Now there is in store for me the crown of righteousness, which the Lord...will award to me on that day, and...to all who have longed for his appearing" (2 Tim. 4:8, NIV)

[21] Strong links have been found between a positive/negative outlook and cardio-vascular disease, cholesterol, and triglycerides. See: ourworldindata.org/data/culture-values-and-society/optimism-pessimism/#health-impact-of-optimism-and-pessimism

> "You rejoice with joy inexpressible and full of glory, receiving the end of your faith—the salvation of your souls" (1 Pet. 1:8-9, NKJV)
>
> "Beloved, now we are children of God; and it has not yet been revealed what we shall be, but we know that when He is revealed, we shall be like Him...And everyone who has this hope in Him purifies himself, just as He is pure" (1 John 3:2-3, NKJV)
>
> "Looking for the blessed hope and glorious appearing of our great God and Savior Jesus Christ" (Titus 2:13, NKJV)
>
> "Therefore gird up the loins of your mind, be sober, and rest your hope fully upon the grace that is to be brought to you at the revelation of Jesus Christ" (1 Pet. 1:13, NKJV)

This alone should be enough to tell us something is off in our perspective of the days ahead. It's time to recalibrate. Readjust.

The 2 Spies vs. the 10 Spies

Pessimism and dread are common today—but they are nothing new. Moses first dealt with them 3500 years ago. When he sent twelve spies into the land of Canaan, what they encountered was not at all what they expected. They found a land of giants and fortified cities, well-armed and prepared for war. Their previous battles had been against a much more provincial foe, nothing like what they now faced. They were *freaked out*. But in reality, they had a huge army, a history of successes, excellent generalship, and *God*. But as they fixated on the problems, they psyched themselves out! Listen to this: "we were like grasshoppers in our own sight, and in theirs" (Num. 13:33). Ten of the spies carried their fear back to the camp and delivered a negative, fearful report full of doom and dread: "*We're all doomed!*" As fear does, it spread like wildfire through the camp.

But the two spies, Joshua and Caleb, knew better. They were experienced warriors, not given to fear. They saw a mighty army and a God who was ready, willing and able to give them the land. They said the giants "will be bread for us" (Num. 14:9).

It is a fitting metaphor for our day. As you will see in Chapters 3 and 5, God is giving us the land. Though I certainly see the "giants" and "fortified cities" ahead of us, I have joined a growing number who are anchoring to the big picture.

I can't emphasize enough how important an overcoming perspective is. God was so dismayed by the fear and doubt of the ten spies, He completely disinherited them. Because of everything He had done on the Israelites' behalf, God expected them to have faith in Him. But instead, they had negative faith – faith in their doom! Dear friends, *a fearful, doomed view simply has no place amongst believers.* Zero. Even if we believe our challenges are overwhelming, we cannot fear. We must be immovably anchored to an overcoming perspective. At its core this book is simply a call to all believers to exit the ten-spies "we are doomed" camp—and get on board with Joshua and Caleb, and be warriors who never yield to fear. We have a big God and a pile of promises.

Maybe the first place we should re-examine is our view of increasing darkness.

CHAPTER 2

Reason #2:

THE WORLD IS GETTING BETTER

> **Fact:**
> **"The path of the righteous is like the light of dawn, that shines brighter and brighter to the full day."**
> **(Prov. 4:18)**

It is a common notion that everything is getting worse, that the world is getting darker. Some might even say that we have crossed the point of no return.

Are things worse than ever before? Is the world only growing darker?

In a word, no. And I'm going to prove it to you.

Numerous statistics and trends suggest that the world is getting better. Why haven't you been told? Because that's not what drives viewership or sells newspapers, books and newsletters! Ironically, this non-virtuous cycle means our only source of information is more negative information, which seems to reinforce the validity of the problem. My goal is to help retrain the church to look at current events through the wider angle of history, and to view this data with new, clean "two-spies lenses" rather than old, tarnished "doom lenses." Why? Because *our expectations color our conclusions*.

Friends, I will say it many times, in many ways, but in Jesus, our future is filled with hope! Christians should be the most optimistic, thriving, persevering, and joyful of all people. If you think the dim flickering candle of poor little Jesus cannot survive the gale force winds of the muscular Satan, then this chapter may be the beginning of a whole new approach to life.

The Facts Speak For Themselves

Is our planet descending into utter darkness? As a student of both economics and history, an engineer by training, a database expert, and an analyst by nature, I decided to find out. I started without prior assumptions, just following the raw data wherever it led. I began assembling every meaningful data stream—sociological, psychological, moral, political, and economic—that was quantifiable and had enough history behind it to generate long-term trends (think centuries and millennia, not months and years). Since Jesus began his ministry in roughly 30 AD, what has changed on earth? For the last twenty centuries, have things gotten generally better or generally worse, and on what scale? I began my quantitative analysis and discovered some amazing trends that have been drastically overlooked in our fascination with despair.

Obviously, this isn't an academic paper, so I can only hit the highlights, but I've summarized progress into the following categories: Wealth, Health and Nutrition, Liberty, Human Rights, Literacy, Law and Safety, Business Ethics, Giving, and Evangelism and Christianity. Get ready for some surprises.

Wealth. We know that for thousands of years most of the world's population has lived in extreme poverty. In fact, century after century, wealth concentrated almost entirely at the top, mostly with the royal class, followed by the aristocratic or elite class, then a small merchant/tradesman/military class, all of which comprised a mere fraction of the total population. The modern notion of a "middle class" was virtually non-existent. The distribution of wealth dropped steeply from a small number of wealthy to the vast population of poor with almost nothing in between.

In fact, up until 1820, only two hundred years ago, we know that 95% of the population lived in poverty, with 85% actually classified in "extreme poverty."[22] It means not having enough to eat and unable to reliably shelter or clothe yourself. Those trapped in extreme poverty live hand-to-mouth, day by day, under the constant threat of starvation and exposure.

In *Figure 3 Share of World Population Living in Poverty*, below, you can clearly see the dramatic reversal in this number. After steadily declining for 200 years, in the last 30 years or so, it suddenly dropped by *half.* By current estimates, the percentage of the global population living in poverty stands around 20%. Considered over the wider scope of history, this is astonishing!

---

[22] Poverty is defined as living on less than two dollars per day, in 1985 dollars, and "extreme poverty" less than one dollar.

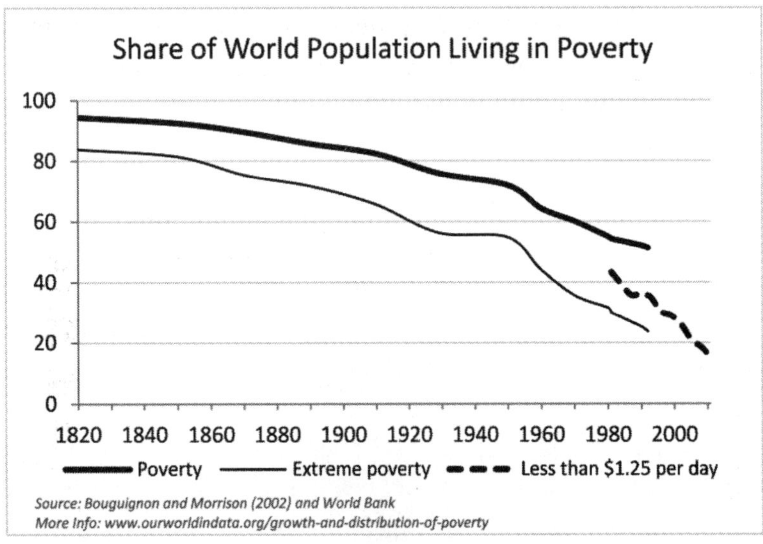

Figure 3 Share of World Population Living in Poverty

Right about now, we need to hit pause and ask ourselves a few questions. Does the enemy want people impoverished? Does Satan like poverty, starvation, premature death, fear, stress, panic? Of course he does! These are works of darkness. By contrast, does God want His children to exist in panic, fear and hunger? No way. He wants people to be prosperous and healthy, for such are the attributes and qualities of the kingdom of light. It was Jesus' idea to care for the poor.[23] Using this measurement, global wealth is being released on a truly historic scale, and global poverty is being eradicated in a measure never before see. This isn't just among rich nations. It is across the globe.

---

[23] Matt. 19:21; Mark 10:21; Luke 14:13, 21; Luke 18:22; Luke 19:8; Rom. 15:26

Does poverty still exist? Unfortunately, yes. Am I content to see poverty at 20%? No, I want it lower still. But I cannot deny one irrefutable fact: *in matters of wealth and poverty, the light is increasing.*

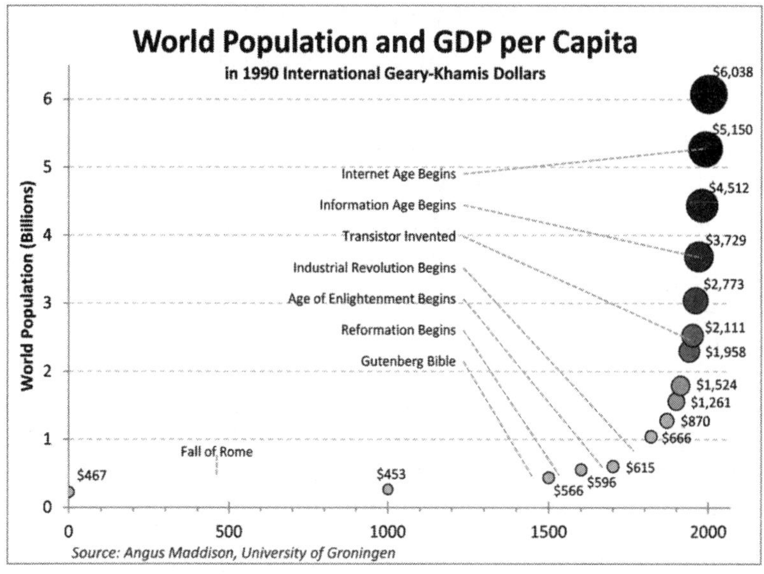

Figure 4 World Population and GDP per Capita

Wealth can best be measured by Gross Domestic Product (GDP) per capita. This number measures the amount of economic wealth created per person. Going back to year one, GDP per capita is pretty flat (see *Figure 4 World Population and GDP per Capita*). Fifteen hundred years, flat. Then, about the time of the Age of Enlightenment, it suddenly began to climb. In the last two hundred years, we've witnessed an exponential surge in population, but real *wealth per person has climbed 13 times faster than population*. Let me ask you, do you have this sort of positive outlook? Is this your frame of reference when you read the headlines with your morning cup of coffee, look at your bills, and contemplate the general fate of the world? Probably not, but it is extraordinarily good news, and you are likely the unwitting recipient of this advancement.

Let's consider another huge, financial positive. Since 1870, 150 years ago, the typical work week was as high as 70 hours across the world. Today, the weekly average is between 35 and 40 (See *Figure 20 Hours of Work per Week, p. 195*). We have this incredible wealth where average citizens now have time to spend with families—a rare luxury not long ago. In other words, most people don't just work to survive anymore. Are you aware? Are you celebrating? Is anybody happy? Because I can assure you, this is way better than working 70 hours a week just to survive? Over the last two centuries, billions of people have come to work less and earn more.

This kind of wealth extends a number of profound benefits beyond the simple elimination of poverty. Among them, it gives dignity to families, as well as providing more diverse options to succeeding generations. This level of confidence and security ripples across the psychological spectrum for men, women and children, translating to further forms of opportunity. In other words, a wealthy, prosperous society is generally better off than a desperately impoverished society. Is that even in question? It's God's heart to give us prosperity. The list of blessings in Deuteronomy chapters 28 make it clear that God's desire and preference is for His people to be the "head and not the tail," "above and not beneath," "to lend to nations and not borrow."

The fact that this is happening in historically, statistically verifiable fashion means one thing: score, light.

But I'm only just getting started.

Health & Nutrition. Hunger and malnutrition were the norm in society until the late 1800s. They were routine in Great Britain and France. Until 1750, the life expectancy in France was 35 years. A typical Frenchman would die in his mid-thirties, mostly due to hunger and malnutrition. The rate was only slightly better in England.

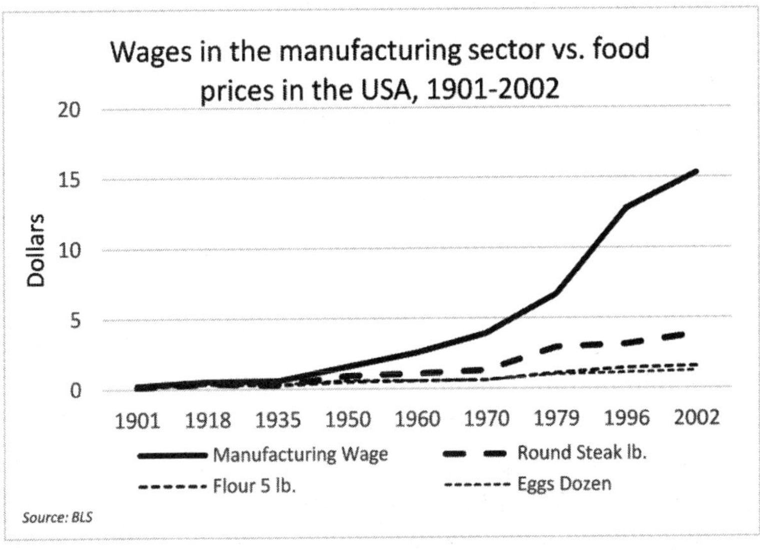

Figure 5 Wages and Food Prices

Look at food prices (*Figure 5 Wages and Food Prices*). Over the last hundred years, hourly wages have steadily increased, while the cost of food has only increased slightly. In other words, the amount of money it takes to feed ourselves and our family has dropped dramatically.

In more good news, infectious disease has largely become an anomaly. If you could travel back in time, this would seem like bizarre, impossibly good news to populations recently devastated by various contagions of the past. So while certain chronic and degenerative illnesses have increased (such as cancer, heart disease and diabetes), the vast majority of plague-level killers have largely been eradicated.

Want more? Deaths in childbirth (see *Figure 21 Maternal Mortality Rates, p. 198*), down by 99% in just 250 years. Child mortality (see *Figure 22 Child Mortality Rates, p. 198*), down. Lifespan, up (see *Figure 23 Life Expectancy, p. 199*). Even in Africa, India and other Third World locales, child mortality is dramatically declining. From the time of the Industrial Revolution to today, the life expectancy of children has increased steadily and dramatically. In 1730, the percentage of London-born children who died before the age of five was a whopping 75%. Mothers, *can you imagine*? Giving birth to four children just to have one live past five years old? Yet this level of death and heartbreak was *normal,* and this is only the childbirth statistic. There were so many ways to die, so much pain and suffering.

And remember, this was only a couple of hundred years ago.

A single breakthrough, penicillin (discovered 1928), while taken for granted today, has literally saved hundreds of millions of lives that would have been lost to various bacterial and microbial infections of the past. During the Age of Justinian, 541-542 AD, the "Black Plague" killed *half the population of Europe* before it finally ran out of steam around 700 A.D. Half. The population of an entire continent suffered for 150 years as a plague ruthlessly and mercilessly eliminated one out of every two persons. Later, the Great Plague of 1347-51 is estimated to have reduced the population of China from 120 million to 65 million. It cost Europe about a third of its population, Africa an eighth (see *Figure 24 Death from Epidemics, p. 199*). Does anybody *really* want to go back? Do you *really* think things are getting worse?

Not to be glib, but let me also inject some levity with two words: Indoor plumbing. Ladies, how many points does the Light Team score just for advances in indoor plumbing and sanitation? So again, I ask, is the world falling apart as we've been told?

That these advances do not exist in a vacuum is the mental "aha!" we need to really shift our way of thinking. Rather, they are part and parcel of what Jesus promised. Christians tend to classify only specifically religious gain as progress, but Satan came to steal, kill and destroy (John 10:10). The bulk of Jesus' ministry was healing the sick. He cares about this! Poverty, death and mayhem are manifestations of darkness, so whenever these things are pushed back, however fractionally, we must learn to recognize that God's heart and values are expanding. When we see advances in wealth, health, safety, etc., by default, that is a divine, not demonic, advancement. Light is encroaching on darkness, not the other way around.

Today, someone can have a heart attack—a heart attack!—and live thirty more years, because we can pull their heart out of their chest, fix it, and stick it back inside them. This is crazy stuff. What's more, the rate of progress and discovery is increasing *exponentially*!

<u>Liberty</u>. Two hundred fifty years ago, the idea that an individual could actually own property, and be protected by law, such that a nobleman or other power could not randomly seize it was a radi-

cal idea. Personal property rights simply did not exist except among the elite. Similarly, to worship according to your conscience, attend the church of your choice, or not attend at all, was not an option. You were told what to believe. You had no choice, no Bill of Rights, and no legal recourse. If you were accused of a crime, you were presumed guilty. You could rot in jail without any hope of a trial. If you were lucky enough to get a trial, it would not be with a jury of your peers. You could marry a wife, but she could be taken at the king's whim. The phrase was *Rex Lex*, which is Latin for "The king is law." In other words, whatever the king says, that's what goes. If he changes his mind, it's like a new law has been written. It doesn't matter if it's inconsistent or unjust. If he wants your land, he takes it. If he wants your bride, he takes her. If he wants to take your business, he takes it. He is the king; he is law.

Only 250 years ago, this was the norm among the nations of the earth.

Then a radical idea developed, sponsored by Christians and theists and a whole group of wildly innovative folks who studied natural law as a revelation of a good Creator who had invested all men with unique and equal worth. These Judeo-Christian ideas formed the bedrock of the wild advancement of American democracy. In the young colonies, a question was raised: what if we built a nation that *governed itself*? The very thought was seditious. It meant the days of *Rex Lex* were numbered. America would be their giant experiment in liberty. But wait! People can't govern themselves! It will be mob-rule, chaos. People need a ruler, a king, a despot.

No, because light was pushing forward. A new day was dawning. Almost with prophetic urgency, a nation "conceived in liberty and dedicated to the notion that all men are created equal; that they have been endowed by their Creator with certain unalienable rights, and that among them is life, liberty and the pursuit of happiness" was born.

But I'm not just cheerleading for America here. Liberty was God's idea right from the start, right there in the garden. Choice and free will, those are His gifts. Jesus came to bring liberty (John 8:36) and abundant life (John 10:10). The "American Experiment" was simply the political expression of God's ways.

Share of World Citizens Living Under Different Political Systems

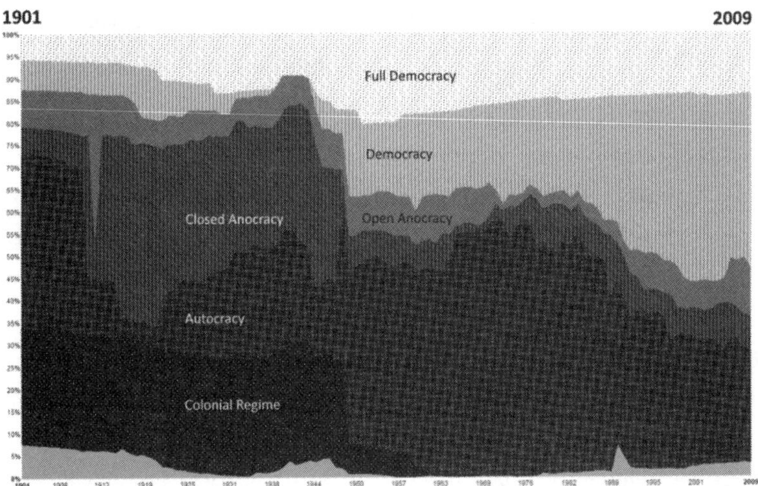

Source: Data on political regimes taken from Polity IV. Population data from US Census and Gapminder
More Info: www.ourworldindata.com

Figure 6 Liberty and Political Systems

These ideas, once considered madness, are now part of mainstream thought. No, they do not exist in every nation, but they dominate the market of ideas. They are part of nearly every prosperous, modern society. The days of despotic kings, tyrants and dictators who perpetuated systemic abuse, graft and theft are waning. Notice in *Figure 6 Liberty and Political Systems* the percentage of the global population under various levels of democracy versus despotism. Today 53% of the global population live under democratic liberty; just 120 years ago, only 12% did. And if we were to look back 250 years, it would be *zero* percent. Freedom of religion, freedom of speech, freedom of thought, are spreading across the globe. That such a titanic shift could happen in just the last century is nothing short of astounding. Liberty is winning, tyranny is losing. Hitler, Stalin, Mao Zedong and every other evil leader have been powerless to stop it. God's ways are advancing in the earth!

<u>Human Rights</u>. The world has seen a huge decline in officially sanctioned human cruelty. This can be measured both in degree and quantity. A thousand years ago, torture-induced confessions were considered a normal function of civil society. Diabolically creative, cruel forms of humiliation and pain were devised and inflicted, as deemed necessary. Human life was cheap. An estimated four to six *million* people died building the Great Wall of China. The emperor simply didn't care. He wanted a wall, so throw more bodies at the problem; there's plenty. The value of each life was largely irrelevant. Today, the United Nations has a Human Rights Commission, and independent bodies like Voice of the Martyr and Amnesty International monitor cruelty on the international stage. This would have been laughable 1000 years ago!

While human rights abuses remain a global problem, the scale of such abuses has declined dramatically. And where they exist, they are being actively opposed and eradicated. This represents an important advance in God's value system, His ways, and His ideas.

Literacy. Two hundred years ago, the world literacy rate was 12%, a terrible figure. Today it's 83% and climbing (see *Figure 25 Literacy Rates, p. 200*). That's progress. Across the globe, literacy rates are improving, which means people are less and less confined to ignorance and superstition. Those excluded opportunity are gaining opportunity. They can educate themselves if necessary. They can read the Bible. Progress, progress, progress.

Law and safety. Ever since the forced signing of the Magna Carta by King John of England in 1215, one of the principal gifts of the British Commonwealth to the world was the growing body of English Common Law. The Magna Carta marked a watershed moment in history, as the erosion of absolute royal power began. Since then, more and more power has been diffused into the people. In keeping with these reforms, the rule of law has also predictably increased.

So, in societies based on the rule of law, corruption is not only frowned upon, it can be investigated and prosecuted. Of course, this remains a rather greasy work in progress. Depending on your city and nationality, various levels of corruption still exist in many sectors of business and government. There's plenty to work on in this regard, but what often goes unappreciated by modern folk is that a certain moral ground has been claimed in the realm of ideas, along with the public implementation of laws that support those ideals. Corruption is now viewed as *negative*, so you can war against it.

Furthermore, in criminal matters, an impressive collection of protections are afforded those accused of a crime: trial by peers, writ of *habeas corpus*, right to a speedy trial, right to the appointment of an advocate, no "double jeopardy," etc. We have civil rights for minorities and equal rights for women. These may seem quaint, and yes, there is still more to be done, but they are revolutionary notions compared to the previous six thousand years of human history.

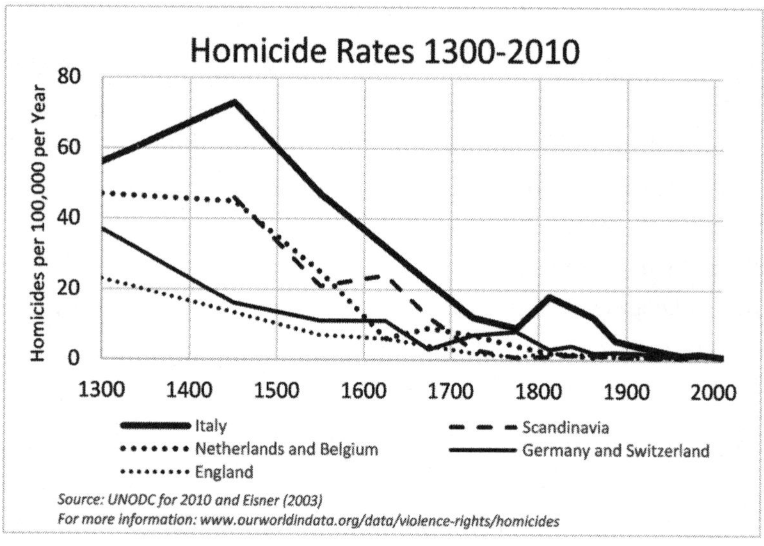

Figure 7 Homicide Rates

Look at *Figure 7 Homicide Rates*. Since 1300, *homicide rates have dropped by 95-99%.* Why? In 1300, no police force existed "to Protect and Serve" the public. Likewise, there was no 9-1-1, no ambulances, no EMTs with defibrillators. Sewage ran in the streets and thievery was a legitimate occupation. Today, law-abiding citizenry and a safe populace are viewed as normal.

Public safety is improving in every dimension. Since the 1900s, the chart below shows the deaths due to natural and technological disasters according to EM-DAT International Disaster Database. While the number of disasters are up, and more people than ever are affected by them (the dashed line), we are seeing *far fewer deaths* (solid line). We're gaining knowledge and making things better, stronger, safer.

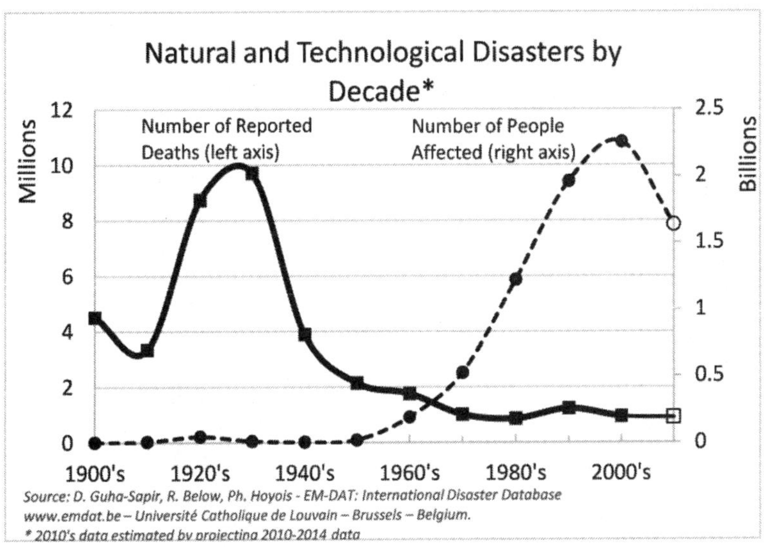

Figure 8 Natural and Technological Disasters

<u>Business ethics</u>. A hundred years ago, exploitive business and labor practices were normal. Innovations during the Age of Steam permitted global titans to flex their powerful monopolistic muscle. Standard operation was to require long hours doing hard labor for little pay, often from an immigrant labor force. Rockefeller, Car-

negie, Morgan, Vanderbilt and others ruthlessly built their empires on the backs of others, rightly earning them the moniker, "robber barons." The nearest comparison is the sweat shops of the Far East today, but these practices are now considered a scandalous affair and any business with ties to such a practice is stigmatized and forced to change their practice. We have laws governing work weeks, child labor and a proper minimum wage to protect people from being taken advantage of, while companies routinely and voluntarily add additional benefit packages including medical insurance and maternity leave.

> Across the globe, Bible principles are now "best practices" in the business world

A guy named John Maxwell is one of world's leading authorities in leadership development for business. He also happens to be a devout Christian whose *modus operandi* is to translate Biblical values into principles for the workplace. Maxwell's teachings are widely considered "best practices" in most major corporations, small businesses and startups around the world. If you go into any business today, they talk about empowerment, valuing workers, creating a positive work environment, loving others, servant leadership, humility, transparency, and integrity. What's the source of all this wisdom? *The Bible*, of course!

Much of this language comes from Maxwell's influence (along with others). And it's worked! Countless human resource department's marketing and mission statements now reflect God's value system. Maxwell was named the number one leadership and management consultant expert in the world by *Inc. Magazine*. Across the globe, Bible principles are now "best practices" in the business world. Though much remains to be done, Jesus' value system has *won the battle* in the realm of ideas. This is remarkable!

Giving. Whether it comes from believers or unbelievers, benevolence is a key indicator of grace at work. Using this metric, the numbers are way up. There are 1.5 million nonprofit organizations in the United States who say their main mission is not to *make* money, but to *help somebody else* or some other group. Where did more than a million generous, giving or benevolent organizations come from? From whose mind? Does that sound like a satanic idea? Let's go help as many people as we can and make nothing for doing it? No! India is home to 3.3 million such organizations. Visit GivingPledge.org and you will discover that 127 billionaires have pledged to give *half* of their wealth to charity. This is staggering! Is such wild generosity the dastardly inspiration of Satan? Hardly.

Evangelism & Christianity. Many consider this the only benchmark, which is why I intentionally put it last, because we're learning the value of additional metrics to judge the spreading influence of the kingdom. Still, this one is key. The gospel is wildly advancing as more missionaries are being trained and deployed across the earth than ever before in human history. Every language and/or people group is slated to have the gospel preached to them within the next 10-20 years. In spite of Communist repression, the last century has seen the gospel deeply penetrate the most populous nation on earth, China.

The knowledge of God is increasing dramatically. In the last one hundred years, concentrations have grown around key revelations.

In the 1500s, Martin Luther restored an understanding of the gospel of grace and the vital role of pastors. In the 1600s, Calvin, Zwingli and the Scottish Presbyterians restored a measure of the role of teacher and a less hierarchical method of church authority. In the 1700s, John and Charles Wesley, George Whitefield, Charles Finney and others restored the ministry of evangelists. Masses came to Christ in waves of revival. In the 1900s and again in the 1950s, we began to see power restored to the church. In the 1960s, the Jesus movement brought new music, authenticity and personal relationship; the 1970s brought the student and youth missions movement, and the Charismatic renewal; the 1980s saw the birth of the fathering movement and the women's movement; the 1990s escalated the prayer movement; and on and on. Each wave brought a new deposit to God's people. This process is not finished. We have a long way to go. But in significant and encouraging ways, we are seeing God strengthen and build His church with truths that are now a part of our spiritual DNA. The average devout believer growing up in 1000AD would not have had a Bible, would have known little of scripture; they would have had none of our understanding of God's power, fathering, discipleship, missions, etc. They would have had little of the true knowledge of God, knowing scant more than superstition and tradition. Look how far we have come.

Have I Lost My Mind?

There are probably a few things going through your mind right now. First, you are realizing that by and large, the world really is a better place, and you are blessed to be here. *It is. You are.* The facts don't lie.

You are probably also racking your brain to think up some negative factors that I missed, or didn't present because I am trying to be positive. Good luck. I didn't selectively "cherry-pick" my data to omit any negatives. In fact I have combed through every data source I could find, and *every* measurable factor with data spanning multiple centuries and geographies shows improvement. I found many negatives of course, but all were too localized (a single nation) or too short term (less than 100 years) to be considered a truly global, big picture trend.

Every measurable factor with data spanning multiple centuries and geographies shows improvement

A common point of concern for many today is the environment. There is a plethora of alarming data on global warming, deforestation, ocean acidification, species extinction, water scarcity, and crop monoculture to name a few. Many of these negative trends span multiple geographies, but only began worsening in 1970's or 1980's. It is too soon to know if it they are really big-picture trends or not. I will cover these more in my blog at *KingdomHorizonBook.com.*

I did find one data point that was a mixed bag: war. In *Figure 14 Global Deaths in Conflict (p. 194)*, I plotted per-capita deaths in conflict by century. On the negative side, 8 of the top 20 most deadly conflicts in the last 2000 years have been in just the last 200 years. War and conflict remain a massive and tragic problem. But the trend is not all negative: per-capita deaths have dropped over time. Madman Genghis Khan's army slaughtered 11% of the population of the *entire globe*; World War II, 3%. Still horrible, but perhaps a positive.

You also might also be thinking I am ignoring the more important *moral* issues: increasing secularism in government and media, increasing sensuality and militant homosexuality; repression of religious liberties, etc. I too am concerned about these issues.

However, as a student of history, I have studied in depth dozens of historical societies. For example: the highly sexualized and corrupt Roman Empire of Jesus' day, where in Pompeii, there were discovered as many as 35 brothels, one for every 71 male citizens,[24] phalluses were carved into the street, into walls, above doorways and bread ovens, and sexualized art was found throughout the city;[25] or the bloodthirsty Vikings 1000 years ago, who mockingly labelled one warrior "Olvir the Child-Sparer" for his laughable mercies in refusing the custom of impaling children;[26] the demonic Mongols and Timurids 700 years ago, who inexplicably wiped out half a continent; the Aztecs 500 years ago, where they found in just one small city a skull rack with upwards of

[24] en.wikipedia.org/wiki/Lupanar_(Pompeii)
[25] www.ancientdigger.com/2012/05/pompeii-erotic-art-and-roman-sexuality.html
[26] *The Saga of Grettir the Strong*, Penguin Books, 2005

136,000 human sacrifice victims.[27] Anyone who claims modern society is more immoral than past centuries is ignorant of history.

Anyone who claims is modern society is more immoral than past centuries is ignorant of history

And though we are seeing a recent increase in secularism, the trend is too short term and too concentrated in western countries to be considered a big-picture global trend. Despite the decline, still 80% of Americans say, "I never doubt the existence of God," 76% say, "Prayer is an important part of my daily life," and 76% also say, "We all will be called before God at the Judgment Day to answer for our sins" (see *Figure 15 Religious Values in the US, p. 195)*.

We have seen a dramatic increase in the acceptance of homosexuality (see *Figure 16 Values vs. Rights in the US, p. 195)*. One would expect to see a proportional decline in traditional values in family and marriage, but in fact we have seen only a slight decline. One can only conclude that changes in attitude regarding homosexuality are not outright approval of homosexual lifestyles, but more related to a growing tolerance for the individual rights of homosexuals.

Finally, most are surprised to learn how many of the recent trends are actually positive. For example, did you know that in America, teenage pregnancies are down 51% and teen abortions

[27] en.wikipedia.org/wiki/Tzompantli

down 66% (see *Figure 17 Teen Pregnancy Rates in the US, p. 195)?* Yet, a case in point to the negative bias in our society, 74% of adults incorrectly believe these rates are the same or worse. The number of abortion providers in the US has dropped by 41% (see *Figure 18 Number of Abortion Providers in the US, p. 196*).

US crime rates too are down by half, though again, 72% believe they are the same or worse (see *Figure 19 US Crime Rates, p. 197*).

In fact, looking at the trajectories of all these positive spheres of influence, one might even be tempted to argue that the kingdom of God is actually advancing across the planet.

CHAPTER 3

Reason #3

GOD'S KINGDOM IS STEADILY ADVANCING

Fact:
"There will be no end to the increase of His government"
(Isaiah 9:7)

So is God's kingdom winning or losing? Darby, the father of modern Dispensationalism, clearly believed the kingdom of darkness would continually advance until it overcame pretty much everything good in the world. Most Christians today agree that darkness is increasing, the Kingdom of God is losing, the earth is consigned to destruction, and this is what the Bible predicts.

Nothing could be further from the truth.

The Kingdom Of God Is Always Described As Increasing

In *every* verse where the Kingdom of God is described across time, it is described as inexorably advancing.

The Parable of the Mustard Seed (Matt. 13:31-21, Luke 13:18-19). "The kingdom of heaven is like a mustard seed...which is the least of all the seeds; but when it is grown it is greater than the herbs and becomes a tree." The Kingdom of God started *small*; it *grew*, almost imperceptibly, *over time*, until it became a *huge tree*.

The Parable of the Yeast (Matt. 13:33-34, Luke 13:20-21). "The kingdom of heaven is like yeast that a woman took and mixed in...until it worked all through the dough." The Kingdom of God again started *small*; it was hidden; it *grew*, almost imperceptibly, *over time*, until it transformed the *entire* batch.

The Parable of the Growing Seed (Mark 4:26-29). The Kingdom of God is described as a crop that sprouts and grows by itself. Again, starting *small*, *growing* almost imperceptibly *over time*, until it is *fully* ripe. But here Jesus introduces timing: "When the grain ripens, he immediately puts it in the sickle because then the harvest has come." The harvest is of course referring to the end of the age. This means *the grain is growing now, in this age*, and the end will not come until the grain is *fully ripened*.

The Advent (Luke 2:11, Isaiah 9:6-7). As you know, the birth of Jesus was met with great celebration, as angels appeared in the skies and sang to the shepherds. This is because baby Jesus entered a prophetic milieu of Old Testament passages regarding the coming Messiah. In Luke 2:11, Gabriel partially quoted one of these, a key passage in Isaiah 9:6-7.

> "For a child will be born to us, a son will be given to us; and the government will rest on His shoulders; and His name will be called Wonderful Counselor, Mighty God, Eternal Father, Prince of Peace. <u>There will be no end to the increase of His government</u> or of peace."

Isaiah is *not* prophesying the final moment, the return of Christ, but something quite different. He says God's government shall *never stop increasing.* It firmly places the expansion of the kingdom into our day, starting at the birth of Christ. From that point on, Isaiah proclaims that the government and peace of Christ will steadily, unceasingly increase.

Daniel saw the same thing, but in even greater detail.

Daniel Sees the Kingdom Of God

In Daniel 2:31-35, Nebuchadnezzar, the ruler of Babylon, had a dream. In this dream, as Daniel tells it,

> "You, O king, were looking and behold, there was a single great statue; that statue, which was large and of extraordinary splendor...The head of that statue was made of fine gold, its breast and its arms of silver, its belly and its thighs of bronze, its legs of iron, its feet partly of iron and partly of clay. You continued looking until a stone was cut out without hands, and it struck the statue on its feet of iron and clay and crushed them...but the stone that struck the statue <u>became</u> a great mountain and filled the whole earth."

A "Stone cut without hands" is a code phrase from the Old Testament that refers to the long-prophesied Messiah, Jesus. Gabriel himself reveals that the four different sections of the statue represent four different kingdoms scheduled to gain ascendency on the earth: Babylon (the head), followed by the Medo-Persian empire (chest), the Greeks (belly and thighs), and finally the Roman Empire (legs). This was precisely the order of the major world empires to come until the little stone was revealed in the days of the legs of iron. Jesus was born in Judea, a tiny little subjugated nation occupied by the fourth kingdom, Imperial Rome.

Now notice one important little word. I underlined it in verse 35 above, "became." A *process* is involved. The stone did not instantly grow into the mountain which toppled the statue and eventually filled the whole earth. It *became* a mountain. Thankfully, Daniel doesn't leave us in the dark on this.

> "In the days of those kings the God of heaven will set up a kingdom which will never be destroyed, and that kingdom will not be left for another people; it will crush and put an end to all these kingdoms, but it will itself endure forever." (vs. 44)

That little stone, seemingly outgunned by so much evil and wrong in the world, will actually break the statue into pieces, then grow and grow even as the statue is completely annihilated, turning to dust and finally blowing away. This refers to everything: the thinking, mindsets, laws, structures and other trappings of the precursor kingdoms.

They won't last. They can't. Only God's kingdom will endure. But the progress of the one, and the failure of the other, doesn't happen all it once. The kingdom of God *becomes*.

The stone becomes a mountain. In scripture, mountains always speak of authority and government. This mountain filled the whole Earth, which evokes the steady, microscopic, day-by-day advance of something that began in the days of the Roman Empire. Jesus was born and crucified with a Latin imprint nailed above his head on a Roman cross, and from that day forth, the Kingdom of God began increasing.

And lastly, Daniel makes it clear this dream describes what will soon take place on the earth. Make no mistake, he says, this dream describes a time-sequence, and it is *literal*—it is not figurative:

> "...the great God has made known to the king what will come to pass after this." (vs. 45)

Here are the main points:

1. The stone is a *literal* empire, as tangible as those preceding it. Jesus' kingdom will literally impact the earth just as the previous kingdoms did.
2. The stone is uniquely *authored by God* in that it was "cut without hands." If there is any question that the stone is symbolic of Jesus, He referred to Himself using this phrase (Mark 14:58).
3. The stone *became* a mountain. It is a process, over time.
4. The stone will overcome all other kingdoms.
5. It will fill the *whole* earth.
6. It will last *forever*.

So we see all these elements of the Kingdom of God: starting *small*, at the birth of Christ in the days of the Roman Empire, then *growing*, slowly, steadily, almost imperceptibly, *inexorably*—which means, *impossible to stop or prevent, relentless, inescapable, inevitable, unavoidable, irrevocable, unalterable*; the Kingdom grows—*until*—it reaches fullness.

So, What Is The Kingdom Of God?

In Chapter Two we showed a plethora of indicators that the world is not growing darker. What I am about to say next may come as a shock.

All the trends shown in Chapter 2, increasing liberty, safety, health, wealth, etc. are, in fact, *manifestations of the Kingdom of God increasing*. It is evidence of the "stone, cut without hands," filling the whole earth, the mustard seed, the leaven Jesus brought, leavening the planet.

When Jesus healed a mute, He explained the action with this phrase, "The Kingdom of God has come upon you" (Luke 11:20). He later said, "The Kingdom of God is within you" (Luke 17:21). Most conclude by this that the Kingdom of God is purely "spiritual" activity in the domain of the human heart.

But digging a little deeper, we find *there is more to it*.

Zacchaeus was a greedy, unscrupulous tax collector. He was not a good man, and like many in his profession at the time, was probably abusing his authority in pursuit of profits. As the story is told in Luke 19:1-10, Jesus approached him and invited Himself to Zacchaeus' house. Zacchaeus was so blown away, so deeply touched, that at the end of the meal he announced, "I am going to change my ways, be a generous man, and make it right with everybody I have wronged!"

Jesus responded, "Today, salvation has come to this household."

This is a remarkable statement, but look at what *doesn't* happen in this passage. No demon was removed, no healing occurred. A *greedy* man became *generous*. That's all. Jesus said salvation entered, which means the Kingdom of God set up shop in Zacchaeus' home.

So then, what exactly *is* the Kingdom of God? The Kingdom of God is anywhere the government of God extends—just as a natural king would describe his kingdom as the extent of his rule. So the *Kingdom* of God and the *government* of God, are the same thing. The Kingdom of God is where the government of God extends.

So when Jesus healed the mute by casting out a demon, the government of God displaced the government of Satan in that situation—thus Jesus called it the Kingdom of God expanding.

And the Kingdom of God is also when the *ways* of God displace the *ways* of Satan. Like when a greedy man becomes generous. When integrity replaces lying, when giving replaces selfishness, when forgiveness replaces bitterness, it is actually the Kingdom of God expanding, because these things are God's ways, not Satan's.

God Cares about His Ways

Because we think of the Kingdom of God solely in terms of spirituality, we focus our efforts on traditional missionary efforts, evangelism, confession of faith, and baptism. This is good—it is step one.

But if an evangelism crusade has a hundred men raise their hands in confession of faith, but then they all go home and beat their wives, has the Kingdom of God really come? *Not so much.* Likewise, if the same crusade preaches a message that brings conviction, and no raises their hand, but a hundred wife-beaters go home and quit beating their wives, then the *Kingdom has come* in measure; God's ways are supplanting the enemy's ways.

Does this negate the need for salvation? Not at all. It simply means we must develop a broader measurement of it. God has always valued *ways* above *words*. Consider the words of Jesus:

> "What do you think? A man had two sons, and he came to the first and said, 'Son, go work today in the vineyard.'
>
> "And he answered, 'I will not'; but afterward he regretted it and went.
>
> "The man came to the second and said the same thing; and he answered, 'I will, sir'; but he did not go. Which of the two did the will of his father?"
>
> "They said, 'The first.'" (Matt. 21:28-31)

Guess what? They were right, a fact which Jesus affirmed. Ultimately, it's not the one who talks the talk, but walks the walk, right? From this verse it is clear, it cannot be said the Kingdom of

God has come until His *ways* are adopted. When His ways come, it can truly be said His kingdom has come.

This is why Jesus emphasized a teaching ministry as much as a power ministry. This is why Jesus made observance of His ways a central part of the Great Commission:

> [19] Go therefore and make disciples of all the nations.... [20] teaching them to observe all things that I have commanded you. Matt 28:19

"Make disciples *of* all the nations" – not *in* all the nations. The mandate is to teach them to practice the "things He commanded"—*his ways.* The emphasis was not on *belief,* but on *applying His teachings*.

Psalm 67 succinctly states the paradigm which should govern our perspective.

> "May God be gracious to us and bless us and make his face shine on us—so that your ways may be known on earth, your salvation among all nations... for you rule the peoples with equity and govern the nations of the earth." (vs. 1-2, 4).

God is committed to His *ways* being known—*adopted*—on earth. God's ways are meant to "govern the nations".

God has *ways*, articulated so well in Jesus' teachings. Love vs. selfishness; forgiveness vs. bitterness, generosity vs. stinginess, truth vs. lying, integrity vs. cheating, and thousands of others. When love replaces selfishness, when kindness replaces cruelty, it can be said the Kingdom of God is expanding. When a CEO picks up a book by John Maxwell and shifts the culture of his company from exploitation to empowerment, the Kingdom is coming. When another billionaire bequeaths half his wealth through The Giving Pledge, the kingdom is coming.

In fact, *they are doing what Zacchaeus did.*

The big-picture trends in Chapter Two show God's value system is growing and being adopted around the world. Human rights, caring for the poor, eradicating sickness—these are all His ideas, and they are winning, over time. It makes sense, because they are better ideas. They work. Peace is better than war. Law is better than murder. Life is more desirable than death. The world is en masse adopting His teachings.

By the way, a sidebar for evangelists: *adopting the teachings of Christ opens the doors to accepting Christ.* Jesus said people's actions, when they are not aligned with God, actually keep them from accepting Christ:

> [20] For everyone practicing evil hates the light and does not come to the light, lest his deeds should be exposed. [21] But <u>he who does the truth comes to the light</u>, that his deeds may be clearly seen, that they have been done in God." (John 3:20-21)

In other words, a person who accepts God's ways is one step closer to accepting God.

God's ways often begin as simple ideas. But they are compelling and they really work. Love works. Generosity works. Servant leadership works. As they gain traction, lesser ideas, Satan's ways, are displaced, and he loses ground. Let's look at one powerful example.

Case In Point: Slavery

Slavery is a terrible part of the human condition, a fact that has existed for millennia. As long as human beings have lived, slavery has been part of human culture. Slavery was routine in our oldest civilizations, including Assyria, Babylon and Egypt. The Code of Hammurabi prescribed death for anyone who helped a slave escape or gave shelter to a fugitive. The Roman Empire partially justified their conquest of new territories in order for the procurement of slaves. We know from history that roughly 20% of the Roman populace was enslaved. This formed part of the economic incentive for warfare.

Slavery was an indispensable part of the labor supply, critical to a functioning economy and maintaining the existing order. It was a fully entrenched cog in the gears of society.

It was a fact of life, universally accepted, and fully justified and legitimized institution for the last 6000 years. Slavery was viewed as *normal*, and even *right*.

Until 200 years ago.

When a movement began.

William Wilberforce, a devout Christian, i.e. a builder of the Kingdom of God, by relentless determination, aided by the prayers and tireless work of many fervent abolitionists, and with great legal cleverness, *overturned the entire institution* in Great Britain. The ripple effects of that single transformation—salvation coming to the house of England, if you will—utterly upended the previously accepted normalcy of slavery across the globe. It started a domino effect across the globe as nation after nation abandoned slavery.

Consider: after six thousand years, in which millions of people suffered the ignominy of slavery, the tides turned roughly two hundred years ago. Today, there is not a soul arguing that slavery is legitimate and moral. Who is the apologist in our day for the moral superiority of slavery? *That's* the point. Nobody is going on CNN or Fox News to advocate that if we really want to fix the economy, we need to return to slavery. *The thinking of the entire planet has shifted 180 degrees, and now agrees with God.* While slavery and human trafficking still exist, they are practiced only by criminals and despots. In the realm of value systems and ideas, God has completely triumphed; the idea-battle is over. Now we are in the "mop-up" phase, stamping out slavery and human trafficking wherever they exist, every single victory of which further expands His kingdom (see *Figure 13 Decline of Slavery, p. 193*).

This transpired in a period of time in which, to Darby's manner of thinking, everything could only worsen. Yet a godly reformer refused such notions and brought God's ways to the planet. I ask you, does Satan like slavery? Of course he does! It is systemic abuse and exploitation of people that destroys lives. Yet from Wilberforce on, the Kingdom of God has invaded that arena, and the terms of engagement have drastically shifted in favor of liberty and equality. Satan can no longer practice it with impunity. Satan is now restrained in this area, by *humans* who adopted God's *ways*. God's ways have been established in that area; His government has increased. His ways have permeated the thinking of humankind and a new normal has been established that makes no allowance for slavery. The kingdom is embedded. It can't easily be removed.

So Good Always Wins, Right?

No, of course not. This doesn't mean the Kingdom of God doesn't ever lose a battle. It doesn't mean that the Kingdom of God is never opposed. It just means that it is always advancing. It keeps growing and growing and growing. It doesn't mean that every branch grows in every place, every time, like a perfectly symmetrical tree. In certain times and places, evil rears its head and darkness surges forward. I think of times like Hitler, or the Black Death, or the communist purges of Christians and scholars. The enemy chops off a branch of Jesus' mustard tree. But the tree endures the barrage, and then continues growing, expanding. A century or two later, you can't even tell a branch was destroyed, and the tree is twice as large.

So does this mean Christians, or the Kingdom of God will take over every aspect of society prior to His return as some purport (many post-millennialists, Kingdom Now, or Dominion Theology in Christian Reconstructionism)?[28] Or is Darbyism correct, which envisions the opposite, a future filled with darkness in which believers are completely overcome?

I'm not a proponent of either view.[29] I believe we should live with hope, not fear; we should act with zeal, invest with vision, and build with passion. We should do this as if it were up to us to bring the kingdom in full with no predefined limits of how far we

28 I am not in any way attempting to create or justify the imposition of a theocracy. The ultimate theocracy is God ruling and reigning when He comes, which will only be possible when He comes. We are not trying to create a theocracy in this age.
29 In Matthew 13, the Parable of Wheat and Tares reveals the maturing process of evil "tares" sowed by an enemy into a field of good "wheat." The presence of tares at the harvest implies evil will exist at the end of the age.

can go or how much we can succeed, all the while knowing that, ultimately, He will finish it when He returns.

It started as virtually nothing. One man, Jesus, son of Mary and Joseph, a single seed among tens of billions of human lives over the course of history. A small stone born during the age of Rome. His life, death, resurrection and teachings were a little part of a little kingdom on this little earth. His tiny life, almost like a speck of dust driven among the mighty winds of empires and time, was too small to register or even matter. Yet here we stand, with the reckoning of history itself divided by His birth, and the nations of the earth overshadowed by His life.

Starting small, growing slowly, almost imperceptible over time, His yeast is spreading, leavening the earth; the mustard seed of His ideas are being increasingly adopted, becoming a mighty tree. His government is ever-increasing. His ideas are consuming other lesser ideas which are part of lesser kingdoms. This will continue until it becomes full, then the end will come. It will fill the whole earth, and it will last forever!

These days are those days—an epoch of gradual, continual, inexorable expansion.[30] While 3,000 people were saved in a single day at Pentecost, roughly 3,000 people are born again across the world *every 25 minutes!* In his book, *Megashift*, author James Rutz says that most Americans don't realize the scale of what's happening simply because Western Christianity is no longer the planet's

[30] Among other passages, see: Num. 14:21; Prov. 4:18; Isa 9:6-7, 54:2-4; Dan. 2:44; Micah 7:11-12; Hab. 2:14; John 12:32; Matt. 16:18; also, the Parable of Leaven; of the Mustard Seed; of the Growing Seed

driving force.[31] A traditional Catholic stronghold like Latin America now has more evangelicals attending church than Catholics attending mass. Mass crusades in Africa have produced tens of millions of believers, while the underground church in China has exploded into the hundreds of millions in a single century. Rutz says this kind of growth is trending toward wholesale, national transformation in various parts of the earth.

"This is the biggest megashift in history. Can you think of any time when over a billion people eagerly changed their lives and loyalties in one generation? …We are in the early stages of a total transformation of our planet."[32]

Rutz goes on to say, "God writes history, but human eyes have trouble reading his handwriting. It's not that he writes too small, but too big."

In influence, populace and reach, the facts agree with the trajectory of scripture. God's kingdom has been steadily growing for two thousand years. As Rutz's data makes plain, this trend has only accelerated. Persecution has not stopped it. Crime, terrorism, immorality, technology, innovation, politics, war, disease, corporate greed, social upheaval, and even competing world religions all continue to exist, perhaps even thrive, in measure, yet they have done nothing to stop the steady increase of God's government and ways.

---

[31] Until 1960, Western evangelicals outnumbered non-Western evangelicals (i.e. Latino, black, and Asian) two to one, but by the year 2000, non-Western evangelicals had surpassed Westerners *four to one*. James Rutz, *Mega Shift: Igniting Spiritual Power* (Colorado Springs, Co: Empowerment Press, 2005), 25-27.
[32] ibid

Fine, you say. Point yielded, but that's not really the issue. What we're really concerned about isn't the slow, steady advance of goodness, but a sudden, total collapse of social order. We all know that, sooner or later, "the system" is doomed to collapse. Right?

Wrong.

CHAPTER 4

Reason #4:

THE SYSTEM IS NOT COLLAPSING

Fact:
"Yet once more I will shake not only the earth, but also the heaven...so that those things which cannot be shaken may remain."
(Heb. 12:26-27)

So what does it mean that everything will shake? Everything will *shake*, but that doesn't mean everything will *collapse*. In fact the main point of the verse is reassurance. So where does our economy fit into that equation? What about the dollar?

Once more, there is more reason to hope than fear.

It's time to turn our attention to "the system," by which I mean the overall machinery of socioeconomic factors, including governmental and financial policy that serve to create a stable society. In their desire to spot signs of the imminent return of Jesus, many Christians have latched onto one doomsday prediction after another. While most surely prefer a stable and prosperous society, there is an expectation of growing instability, ending with economic and societal collapse. It is welcomed as a sign of the coming end.

But in fact this is a completely wrong-headed idea.

Do you realize that *Jesus described His coming as being in the midst of routine, normal life*? When He compared His return to the days of Noah, He described people "eating and drinking, marrying and giving in marriage, up to the day Noah entered the ark" (Matt. 24:38). Then He adds this little detail, "This is how it will be at the coming of the Son of Man" (vs. 39). Luke 17:28 adds, "Buying, selling, planting, building." Eating, drinking, marriage, business. *Normal life*. Crazy, huh? Is that what you expect? Since it directly contradicts the extreme picture painted by some, such explicit, red-lettered normalcy should get our attention. We get hyped by the hype of some terrifying, extreme future, but Jesus stated precisely the opposite. If you envision the earth as a nuclear wasteland where post-apocalyptic gangs trade gasoline for scraps of food, I'm not sorry to say, you will be disappointed.

You, Me and Mad Max

In this chapter, I'm going to present cold, hard facts to address what I call the Mad Max scenario. Should a Mad Max endgame occupy a place in the Christian arsenal either for the sake of apologetics or wise, practical preparation? If you saw the Mel Gibson cult classic from 1979, you know the entire plot of the movie revolved around nondescript devastation in some not-too-distant future. The Mad Max world had no society, per se, only lawless, roving motorcycle gangs and violent thugs driving tricked-out, armored automobiles. Human factions fought constantly to control limited basic resources: food, water, fuel, safety. That's the plot: Darwinian desperation, crime, and explosions.

Dystopian visions of the future awaken nearly every primal fear a person could face, especially for parents who rightly want to protect their children from harm. In response, an entire movement of "preppers"—Christian and non-Christian alike—have undertaken various strategies, including the stockpiling of dried and canned foods; water purification techniques and gardening (not for the joy of gardening, but for survival); hoarding staple, tradable items like duct tape, Band-Aids and salt; learning field craft and wilderness skills; amassing guns and ammo. It's Mad Max, minus the violence. So far.

As part of this, sermons encourage neighborhoods to rally together with a common plan. In urban centers, people have "go bags" in their closet, stuffed and ready with quick, short-term necessities, and an escape route plotted should the go bag be necessary. Mad Max scenarios include biological and nuclear warfare, terrorist violence, racial riots, natural disasters leading to food shortage, and the total collapse of currencies, all of which could lead to martial law. We have normalized a certain threshold of fear and live with that expectancy, therefore we feel *slightly* safer thanks to our preparations. No doubt, it can certainly be a wise precaution. A basic emergency preparedness plan is definitely a smart choice for people in every period of time, in virtually every location.

But that's not what we're talking about.

The real question is whether the Mad Max scenario will be the inevitable conclusion of civilization? Are time, sinfulness, Calvinistic fate (and maybe the Illuminati) conspiring to crack the floor joists of social order and collapse the entire structure?

For decades, this view was part of my thinking. After extensive research, I have become persuaded otherwise. Allow me to show you why I no longer share this view.

Economic Collapse Scenarios

Perhaps the biggest "total collapse scenario" revolves around economic collapse. Many folks expect this to occur in the very near future. Quite literally, they're banking on it by making investment decisions (or non-decisions) governed by the belief that the stock market and currencies will fail. Back in the days when I subscribed to this point of view, I read a number of books that fueled my outlook. Most are still on my bookshelf! I will show you a few on the coming pages. One is titled, *Bankruptcy, 1995*. Obviously, note the year. The book predicted that in the year 1995 "America will enter an age of financial disaster that will dwarf the Great Depression and hail the end of the United States as we now know it."

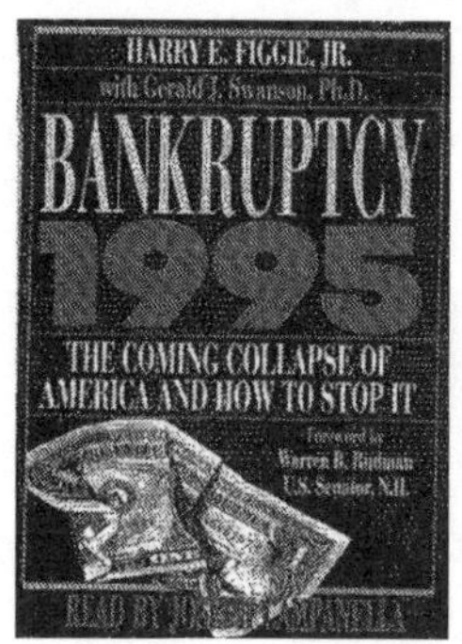

This was preceded by a deeply researched book from the late Larry Burkett, a godly man and an astute economic adviser. His book, *The Coming Economic Earthquake,* was Book of the Year in

1992. He predicted that the national debt would be monetized (it happened, partially) and that it would result in "a calamity not seen since the Great Depression" (didn't happen). These and other titles were penned by sincere, intelligent, principled people, not opportunists or fear-mongers. Many were believers. Fortunately, they had one thing in common: they were all wrong. I'm not mocking, I'm observing. That's the benefit of hindsight.

Will we possibly see various manner and levels of financial disruption in the future? Of course! Some of it could get pretty ugly. We know that as a matter of record because it's happened hundreds and hundreds of times before. One of my favorite books on this topic is titled, *This Time Is Different*, by Carmen Reinhart and Kenneth Rogoff. The authors looked at 800 years of financial crises. Did you know that there have been 265 major financial crises in 66 countries over the last 800 years? The point: it happens, let's deal with it.[33]

Most financial collapse forecasters underestimate several factors: the power of humans to adapt, the power of technology, the power of innovation and the power of central banks and the government. If you are reading this book, it means you have lived through one of the most severe economic crises in the last hundred years. While some would argue we have not yet fully emerged

---

[33] One of the book's main points was that high levels of public debt result in lower economic growth. Calculation errors were discovered in 2013 that showed this conclusion was incorrect. However, I successfully used other areas of research from this book to correctly predict the depth and duration of the 2008-12 housing crisis and banking crisis. My point here is that financial crises are both common and survivable.

from the recession of the early 2000s, it was nevertheless amazing to see bankers, central bankers, and the government focus on doing whatever was necessary to save the economy. My background is as a fiscal, political and social conservative, so here's a confession that few from my wing would be willing to make: By and large, they succeeded.

Cycles Down, Cycles Up

These cycles are part of the human economy, so let's look at a few quick summaries, decade by decade. Though I have vastly oversimplified for the sake of space, my larger points will be fairly self-evident.

1970s. By all indications, financial Armageddon and debt collapse should have happened in the 1970s. When we departed the gold standard in 1971, gold began to skyrocket and the dollar fell. In response, the oil-producing nations (OPEC) decided to price oil in terms of gold, and then the Arab oil exporters embargoed oil exports to the US in retaliation for US support of Israel in the Yom Kippur war. Oil shortages paralyzed the nation, oil prices skyrocketed, and inflation followed. As a nation, we were already reeling from the political, moral and economic cost of Vietnam, riding waves of powerful disenfranchisement from the 1960's. Then it got worse: Watergate, the 1973-74 stock market crash and the Iran hostage crisis. Everything was quite desperate (remember, this is the decade of Hal Lindsey's, *The Late, Great Planet Earth*). However, instead of collapsing, the system adapted. Natural gas, cheap and abundant, started replacing oil. Alternative (green) energy innovations gained momentum. Breakthroughs in energy efficiency and conservation significantly began reducing demand. And a guy invents a little silicon chip called the microprocessor, beginning the computer revolution. Against all odds, the economy rebounds.

1980s. We should have seen another collapse in the 1980s, but oil recovered, Reaganomics worked (sort of), and Japan revolutionized manufacturing with a little something known as Total Quality Management (TQM). All over the planet, manufacturing operations became leaner and more profitable, at the same time empowering workers. Concurrently, the personal computer revolution ignited global productivity and put a computer on everyone's desk. Global productivity blew through the roof. None of the doomsayers saw it coming.

1990s. As mentioned above, *Bankruptcy, 1995* and *The Coming Economic Earthquake* were typical of the alarms sounding in the 1990s. Another was *The Great Reckoning: How the World Will Change in the Depression of the 1990s*, by James Dale Davidson. Do you remember the 1990s? Did those things happen? No, the internet happened instead. It ignited a global transformation second only to the industrial revolution of the 1800's. The 1990s were one of the fastest-growing economic decades in human history. I actually built a massively successful technology company in the 1990s!

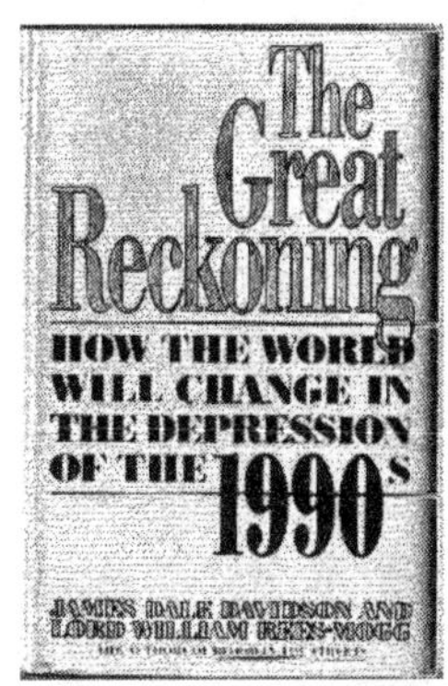

2000s. You can almost see where this is going, right? Sure, crises were averted, but big deal, because it's just compounded our problems. Grim predictions multiplied, rolling off the presses with titles like: *Crisis Economics, Fault Lines, Liar's Poker, Fool's*

Gold, House of Cards, Freefall, Reckless Endangerment, Crash of the Titans, Aftershock, On the Brink, and The Great Rebalancing. The most challenging part of the writing process was likely isolating the best new angle for recycling the fear. Remember Y2K? All the computers were going to stop working in the year 2000. Almost twenty years have passed. Y2K was a blip on the radar, along with every other Mad Max prediction.

The Oil Armageddon

While a decade-by-decade summary is helpful, let's look at a particular trend as a case in point. For those in the know, one of the most compelling Mad Max scenarios involved the perils of "Peak Oil," defined as the point in time when world demand would surpass world supply of crude oil—a critical, finite resource. Oil production had entered a period of terminal decline. For obvious reasons, this was a *big* deal, and intuitively, it makes sense. More alarmingly, we had statistics to back it up. Oil production did in fact peak in 1970 as predicted (in 1956!), and was declining right on schedule.

Until recently, Peak Oil was assumed by many experts to be a foregone conclusion. Since the world quite literally runs on oil, you can imagine the panic and havoc if it ran out. Peak Oil would single-handedly trigger global economic meltdown as every economic sector that depended on oil (which is to say, everything) crashed. Anyone who denied it had their head in the sand. Worse, America, an oil import-dependent nation, was especially vulnerable. Henny Penny was right. The sky was falling. Then a funny thing happened on the way to disaster.

It didn't happen.

Instead, in that same period of time, the oil industry responded creatively to the threat. They developed horizontal drilling and hydraulic fracturing (i.e. "fracking"), releasing billions of barrels of previously unreachable oil. Feel free to question whether fracking poses other geological or environmental risks. Those may be legitimate concerns, but they fall outside the scope of this line of inquiry. Peak oil went in reverse. Look at *Figure 9 Peak Oil Prediction vs. Actual Production.* The black line shows US oil production in the lower 48 states perfectly tracking Hubbert's peak oil prediction (grey line)…until suddenly, it doesn't.

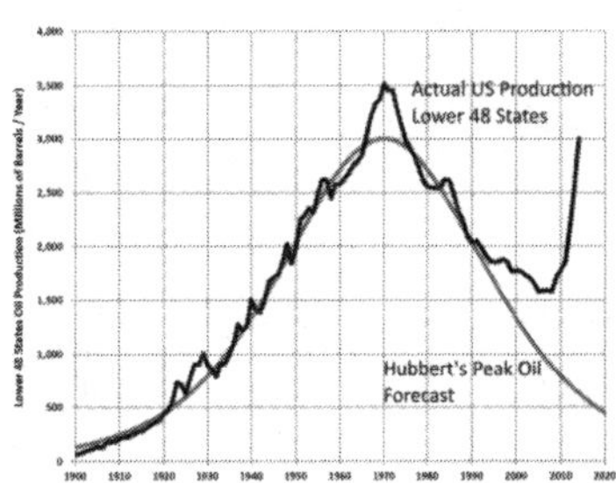

Figure 9 Peak Oil Prediction vs. Actual Production

Meanwhile, in the same span, Texas, Kansas and many more states have begun constructing thousands and thousands of massive wind turbines that is abundant, inexpensive, clean and renewable. Guess what? America is now on track for energy independence in twenty years and, as of 2015, industry trade papers are faced with a new concern: the price of oil is going to go *too low*!

Talk about a switcheroo!

Almost comically, the pundits are already lining up for *cheap oil* to be the new crisis. And so it goes. Because with Henny Penny, the sky was never the problem, Henny Penny was the problem. The real issue is human nature. Nobody wants to be the Pollyannic fool, the dupe. Fear has a built-in audience.

But you and I, we're supposed to be of a different DNA. Hope, rather than fear, should be welded to our soul. When others see clouds, we should see silver lining, and even sunlit fields where clouds are no more,[34] because that is the power of faith, which is the "substance of things hoped for" (Heb. 12:1).

Fear Factors

With all this positivism, am I one of those Pollyannic dupes? Not at all. I am a scientist, and a realist. There are many troubles in the world, a fact abundantly confirmed by negative trends and statistics in many sectors of society that have yet to conform to God's ways. I don't need to convince you of the challenges we face, whether they be cyclical or seemingly permanent. Economies inflate and deflate, industries collapse, progress simply stalls. Regardless, we can stick our head in the sand and wish away our troubles, or confront them head on. My point is this: *negative facts are not necessarily negative*, since research into these unfavorable trends often leads to the next innovation.

For example, would alternative energy solutions be viable options today if they weren't in some sense driven by the peril of the 1970's oil crisis? Probably not. The crisis precipitated the oppor-

[34] "God, you did everything you promised, and I'm thanking you with all my heart. You pulled me from the brink of death, my feet from the cliff-edge of doom. Now I stroll at leisure with God in the sunlit fields of life." Ps. 56:12-13 (MSG)

tunity. Fear factors are real, but *they aren't the whole story.* Doomsday speculations based on "facts" are nearly always based on static models and rarely account for humanity's God-given dynamism, adaptability, creativity and innovation.

As we blaze through the 21st century, several breakthroughs continue to spoil the doomsayers' paranoia party. During a decade of intense recessionary pressures, the internet boom created new industries, jobs and opportunities. Those who chose to invest in the system rather than bail on it, prospered, some quite dramatically. Millionaires and billionaires have been produced in the very same period in which many predicted the dollar would collapse.

Since 2000, the cellular phone revolution produced a smartphone revolution.

Asia is producing legions of engineers and medical doctors, massively scaling humanity's overall capacity for scientific progress.

The human genome has been mapped.

Moore's Law has continued unabated in computer chip technology.

We are in a golden age of discovery in astrophysics and quantum physics. Radical new discoveries are being announced every few weeks.

Dynamic breakthroughs are occurring almost weekly in pharmaceuticals, materials science, digital imaging and green energy. Mass production of electric, hybrid automobiles is no longer the stuff of science fiction, but already here.

Yes, the journey has involved many ups and downs. We've also had the Dot-Com bust. Housing bust. The derivatives scare. The Euro crisis. Enron. Bernie Madoff.

A wild ride, for sure.

And yet, with all that pressure, no Mad Max crash. Fifty years of wild rides, and still no Mad Max. Maybe it's time to change our expectations.

Will The Dollar Collapse?

The collapse of the US dollar is a well-worn narrative that continues to be recycled year after year. *The Death of Money,* by James Rickards is one example. The premise usually revolves around reckless government spending, unsustainable national debt, or the dollar losing its status as a reserve currency.

By way of rebuttal, I will ask one simple question: if you had a billion dollars, which currency would you put it in? The Russian Ruble? Or perhaps the Politburo-controlled Chinese Yuan? Maybe not? How about the troubled Euro? Or the tiny Swiss Franc? What dollar crash pundits always miss is the fact that the only way to price currencies is relative to each other. So if the dollar crashes, it means its exchange rate with other currencies drops—which means the other currencies have to go up in relative terms. All the wealth held in US dollar assets would have to go somewhere else. Where would it go? There is simply no currency that can replace the dollar. Most alternatives are *troubled*, and *all* are too small.

Secondly, the price of anything, including currencies, are driven entirely by supply and demand. If supply is abundant and demand is slack, the price will drop. If supply is steady and demand strong, the price will rise. Dollar collapse proponents see dollar supply increasing through government spending. But as with most doomsday scenarios, the math is off. Demand is the other side of the value equation, and something very few of the dollar doomsday proponents look at. Demand for dollars is created by economic activity, trade, investments, and taxes.

The US has the largest GDP[35] in the world, a fact which is unlikely to change anytime soon, and all this economic activity creates demand for dollars.

Global trade also drives dollar demand: if anyone wants to trade with America, *they still need dollars to do it.* US equipment, iPhones, technology, farm goods—simply put, we have stuff the world wants. In industry after industry, the US is a powerhouse, and that is simply not going to change anytime soon. All of which require dollars. Add to that a recent resurgence in US manufacturing driven by ultra-cheap natural gas energy, and a decline in oil imports due to surging US production, and you have a recipe for a strong dollar.

Furthermore, America remains the world's top investment destination with—by far—the world's largest stock market and the

[35] China has surpassed the US as the largest economy on a PPP basis, but on a dollar basis, my preferred measure, the US economy is about double China.

world's deepest bond market, backed by a robust legal system, rule of law, and high standards of corporate accounting and oversight. For large investors, the US remains the largest and safest of bets.

To argue for the dollar's demise, you would have to argue that the US economy will fail, demand for US goods will drop, and demand US stocks, bonds and real estate will end. As long as America exists as a nation, it's simply not going to happen.

Short version: the dollar is not doomed to destruction.[36] Personally, I believe the dollar will continue to be one of the strongest currencies well into the next decade.

Furthermore, dollar crash proponents miss another key element of currency weakness: a weak currency boosts exports and foreign investment by making them cheaper. This is why countries like China, Korea and Japan are aggressively trying to weaken their currencies today. For the sake of argument, let's say the US dollar dropped by half. That means a European could buy an iPhone for half the cost of a Samsung; or they could buy a Miami beachfront condo for half-price. What would happen? iPhone sales would explode, as would Miami beachfront condos! And they would have to buy dollars to do so, increasing the value of the dollar.

As I write this book, the concern is that the dollar is going to lose its reserve currency status to the Chinese and that will collapse the economies of the world. Frankly, even as the Chinese currency gained reserve status, it's a non-event. An in-depth, detailed analy-

---

[36] Equally obvious, currencies are neither immune to risk, nor stupidity. Citizens should unflinchingly question our elected leaders for recklessly eroding the economy through foolish spending, poor fiscal policy, unfair taxation, corporate loopholes, lack of support for small business, and poorly negotiated international trade agreements.

sis of economics and currencies is beyond the scope of this book, but something I write a lot about. For the latest analysis of currencies and economic trends visit my blog at *KingdomHorizonBook.com.*

Let me quickly highlight a few more aspects that easily get lost in all the "dollar collapse" talk.

<u>The national debt and unfunded liabilities</u>. America has somewhere around $18 trillion in debt, and, depending on how you count it, $200 to $300 trillion more in unfunded liabilities. These are future-oriented promises the government has made that cost money. The big three are Social Security, Medicare, and federal pensions. While these numbers are alarming, yet even here, faced with such massive figures, the sky isn't falling as predicted. Here's why.

With regard to unfunded liabilities, Social Security and Medicare will of course run out of funding at some point in the coming decades. But that doesn't mean national bankruptcy—it means the existing *promises simply will be changed.* The liability gets wiped away because the promise gets changed.

Recent studies have shown that most of the "Millennial Generation" are preparing for retirement by planning and investing without the expectation that the government will take care of them in their old age. [37] It hearkens back to the more self-reliant version of America that existed pre-FDR. If they really *do* prepare for that day, it could significantly relieve the public burden.

---

[37] Only 8% expect full Social Security benefits, while 51% expect none at all. investmentwatchblog.com/millennials-have-got-one-thing-right-only-8-expect-full-social-security-benefits-51-expect-none/#AA7SLXsxRSP1zJOu.99

All these programs, especially Medicare, desperately need to be revamped. It is absurd that US health care spending per capita is double every other nation on earth. And while reform might be jarring, it will not be the end of the *dollar* or the *government*. In spite of the more inane conspiracy theories floating around out there, the United States has no legitimate interest in bankrupting itself.

As for the national debt, history says it can be beaten. The same Harvard economist who wrote "This Time is Different," also studied the countries in history whose debt load exceeded the size of their economy (debt to GDP ratio greater than 100%). Surprisingly, they discovered that only rarely did those countries default on their debt. Instead, they solved their debt problem through a combination of low interest rates and moderate to high inflation. It had side effects, but the system continued. And in cases where the nation did default (meaning they did not pay the debt as agreed, but changed or shrunk the terms), it never "fatally" damaged the country.

But that was in the age of the gold standard. Today even more powerful options are on the table.

Of our $18 trillion national debt, the Federal Reserve currently owns roughly $4 trillion of that total. This happened during the 2008-12 financial crisis, when the central bank created money and bought the debt through its "Quantitative Easing" (QE) program. The debt was "monetized"—the bugaboo of the currency doomsayers—but much to their surprise, the system didn't collapse.

Tomorrow, the Fed could say, "We forgive all that debt," and our national debt would be slashed by almost 25% to $14 trillion.

While such radical action would certainly elicit a collective gasp of concern, it would have *zero* economic consequence. Furthermore, what's to keep the Fed from buying the remainder of the debt and forgiving it too? Having a sovereign currency, and debt issued in that currency, gives the government enormous power and flexibility. Simply put, *the national debt is not going to force America's premature demise*. Again, I can only cover so much in this book; for more details visit *KingdomHorizonBook.com*.

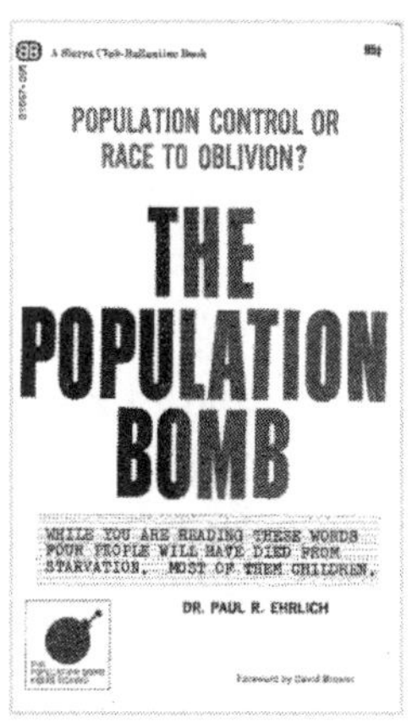

Agriculture. Panic punditry has predicted widespread famines for years, mostly revolving around the supposed inability of our fixed land mass planet to meet the food needs of our burgeoning world population. A predecessor to this fear was the so-called "population explosion," which was a huge worry in the 1960's and 1970's. In 1968, the bestselling book, *The Population Bomb*, through twelve printings, popularized a notion of mass starvation that prevailed well into the 1980's. *The New York Times* called it a "welcome handbook on what is undoubtedly our planet's most serious problem."[38]

If you weren't around in the 1970's you can't appreciate the sheer panic this book brought to the world. Media outlets, universities, scientists, and politicians responded with alarm. It became a common topic of concern amongst the everyday citizenry. Author Paul Ehrlich predicted by the year 2000 famines of Biblical proportion would decimate entire populations, the world's natural re-

[38] Bayard Webster, "Books of the Times: The Population Bomb, by Paul Ehrlich," The New York Times, 1969.

sources would be used up, and the world would be embroiled in constant global war as a result. Amongst other things, he called for government to encourage abortions. The ramifications were horrifying. Yale Law School's Linda Greenhouse and Reva Siegel credited this book as one of the driving forces behind the U.S. Supreme Court's legalization of abortion in 1973.[39] Supreme Court Justice Ruth Bader Ginsburg confirmed the same.[40]

Well, the population bomb hit, but never exploded.

Instead, crop yields *tripled* (see *Figure 10 World Grain Production*, next page). Biotech advances have now created grain crops that yield three harvests a year in Brazil. Rice has been engineered to survive flooding, a major weakness of the crop because there is so much flooding in major rice-producing sectors of Asia. These crops are feeding millions more than standard crops. Our ability to feed people has advanced, not diminished. You may not like GMO's, but they're feeding the world. Thousands of people that would have starved in past generations are now eating.

Even better, prices are lower (after adjusting for inflation) than ever before. Thanks to technology, crop diversity and production going global, prices have stabilized. In previous generations, a bad grain harvest in America would have caused global prices to skyrocket. But when terrible droughts struck America over the last decade, did prices go through the roof? No. The reason is because Brazil has become one of the greatest grain-producing nations on earth, along with the Ukraine, Russia, and China. So if weather

---

[39] Linda Greenhouse & Reva B. Siegel, "Before Roe v. Wade: The Voices That Shaped the Abortion Debate Before the Supreme Court's Ruling," Kaplan Publishing, 2012

[40] Emily Bazelon, "Talking to Justice Ruth Bader Ginsburg," Slate.com, October 2012

patterns are bad here, they are oftentimes good somewhere else. Prices normalize, even in bad years, as technology advances in production, silage, disease-resistance and shipping keeps grain moving between nations. We can weather the weather and continue to feed the population of the earth.

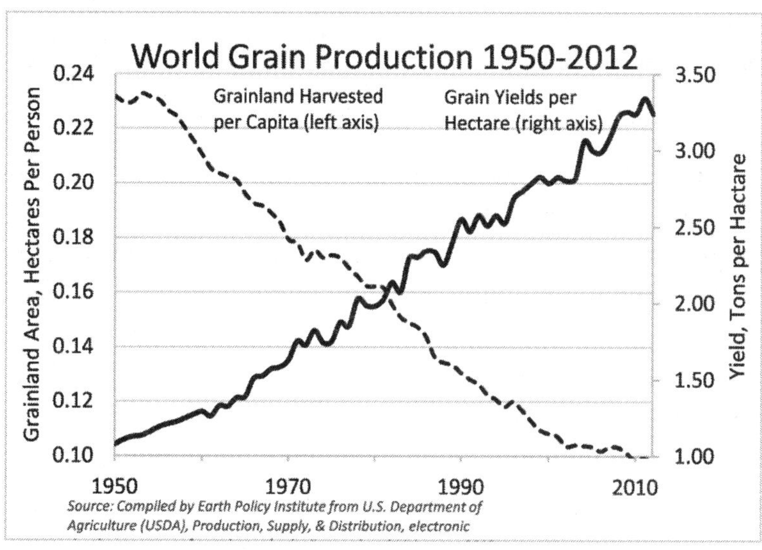

Figure 10 World Grain Production

The Power Grid. This is a popular one, with a list of risk factors ranging from natural to man-made. The worst Mad Max scenario involves a rogue nation setting off a well-placed EMP (electromagnetic pulse) bomb, essentially blasting us back to a medieval lifestyle. The alternative scenario involves a solar storm (a CME, or Coronal Mass Ejection) that blasts the earth with essentially the same effect. The nation's interconnected power grid and our entire electronic/computer-based infrastructure simply fries, blacking out the nation and taking decades to repair.

A friend of mine was part of the North American Electric Reliability Corporation (NERC). This think tank of top scientists and power-grid engineers studied the likelihood of a solar storm wiping out the U.S. power grid. While it is still debated, their conclusion was that a few poorly maintained, older transformers might be destroyed, but the effect on the overall power grid would be completely manageable.[41]

So here we are, nearly fifty years after a gauntlet of disasters spelled certain doom for the world: whether the population bomb, the demise of the gold standard, the oil crisis, computers gone amok, or economic collapse. Instead, world real-GDP per capita has nearly doubled in this span. Perhaps it's time to lay our fears to rest and engage our advancing planet.

While I have shown that most of our fears are exaggerated, I can't promise a future free of terrorism, economic collapse, war, or any other disaster. The truth is that there will always be a crisis, just as there has always been. You will always have reason to fear, but that doesn't mean you should. Crises will come and crises will go; some we'll avert and some we'll endure—but we will advance regardless. And so will the Kingdom of God. It's time to stop basing our lives on fear, and get on with it.

But what about an even larger question regarding the future of the planet itself: Will our planet even be here? What about the simple fact that the Bible says earth will pass away?

---

[41] See "High-Impact, Low-Frequency Event Risk to the North American Bulk Power System" online at www.nerc.com/pa/CI/Resources/Documents/HILF%20Report.pdf

CHAPTER 5

Reason #5

PLANET EARTH IS CENTRAL TO JESUS' ETERNAL PLAN

Fact:
"The LORD shall be King over all the earth"
(Zech. 14:9)

Third Rock from the Sun

If you're like most Christians, this is what you think about Earth: Earth is temporary, this life is temporary, only Heaven is eternal. Intentionally or unintentionally, we place less value on material reality, which leads us to wistfully say things like, "Earth is not my home"—a phrase we invest with deep meaning and emotion, because we are convinced this is really how God wants us to think.

Newsflash #1: It's not.

Hang with me. We know that when we die we go to Heaven. This is biblical (2 Cor. 5:8). However, we also think the "afterlife" refers to an eternity in heaven in the context of a destroyed earth.

Newsflash #2: Wrong.

For most Christians, the future of the planet is a hopeless muddle. Let's break it down.

Earth Belongs To God, but He Gave It to People

Psalm 24:1 says, "The earth is the Lord's, and all it contains." That means everything in, on, under and above the earth belongs to God. Nature, soil, oceans, continents, mountains, crops, weather, rivers, minerals, plants and animals.

All of it. Earth.

Because God owns the earth, He can give it to whom He chooses. He gave charge of the earth to humanity. God created male and female in His image, then told them to increase, steward the earth and exercise dominion over it.

Do not miss this point. He *entrusted* them. He entrusts us with the earth, today.[42] The commission to Adam and Eve continues through you and me.

---

[42] As stewards, we need to take care of our planet and work constantly for clean and sustainable use of our natural resources. The earth is not our "mother," and it is not to be worshipped, but it is beautiful, created by our Father, and entrusted to us. While the earth has been given to us for our use, that is not an excuse for reckless treatment.

"Be fruitful and multiply, and fill the earth, and subdue it; and rule over the fish of the sea and over the birds of the sky and over every living thing that moves on the earth." (Gen. 1:28).

The Hebrew word for "*subdue*" means to *make subservient* and *dominate*. Why? Because the earth is God's, and He is coming back for it. In many of Jesus' parables, He is a landowner[43], and one who departs for a time, but returns to reclaim what is his.

Jesus and His Entourage

Most Christians get this right, that Jesus is returning bodily to the planet. When Jesus ascended, the angels declared to those present that he would one day return physically, bodily, in precisely the same manner as His ascension:

"Men of Galilee, why do you stand gazing up into heaven? This same Jesus, who was taken up from you into heaven, will so come in like manner as you saw Him go into heaven." (Acts 1:11)

But do you know who else Jesus is bringing with Him? *All* the saints, past and present, are coming with him:

[13]...at the coming of our Lord Jesus Christ with all His saints. (1 Thessalonians 3:13, NKJV)

[14]For if we believe that Jesus died and rose again, even so God will bring with Him those who sleep in Jesus. [15]We who are alive and remain until the coming of the Lord will by no means

[43] The parable of the workers, Matt 20:1-16; the parable of the tenants, Matt. 21:33-45, Mark 12:1-9, Luke 20:9-19; the parable of the fig tree, Luke 13:6-9; the parable of the talents, Matt 25:14-30; the parable of the minas, Luke 19:11-27

precede those who are asleep. (1 Thessalonians 4:14-15, NKJV)

That's right!

You. Me. And everyone else who preceded us to heaven.

So, if you die and go to heaven, it is just temporary until Jesus comes back.

Here's another shocker: All the angels are coming too:

[31]"When the Son of Man comes in His glory, and all the holy angels with Him, then He will sit on the throne of His glory. Matthew 25:31 (NKJV)

So, heaven is emptying itself onto earth. What's going on? What is this all about?

Kingdom Earth

Jesus is coming to set up His kingdom on earth. He is bringing is His royal court with Him, His saints and angels, and He is setting up His eternal throne *on the earth*. Yes, you read that right: on earth. Read the verse above again: the "throne of glory" is clearly on the earth after His return. From this earthly throne, He will separate the earthly nations, and then begin His earthly reign. There are many verses that unequivocally declare an earthly reign for Jesus. [44]

[9]And the Lord shall be King over all the earth. (Zech. 14:9, NKJV)

---

[44] Dan 7:13-14; Zech 14:9; Luke 1:32-33, the "throne of David" is an earthly throne; Luke 11:2; Habakkuk 2:14; Num 14:21; Rev 21:3, Rev 11:15; Eph 1:9-10; Luke 13:29; Mark 14:25; Luke 22:18

> [15]Then the seventh angel sounded: And there were loud voices in heaven, saying, "The kingdoms of this world have become the kingdoms of our Lord and of His Christ, and He shall reign forever and ever!" (Rev. 11:15)

Heaven on Earth

When Jesus taught His disciples to pray, His instruction contained this powerful phrase, "Your kingdom come, your will be done, on earth as it is in Heaven" (Matt. 6:10).

Often missed in this prayer is the point of view. The point of the prayer is the transformation of earth to more fully resemble heaven, which is to say, increase His earthly government.

God made it clear from the beginning that earth, eventually, would fully express His kingdom, values and power. "The earth will be filled with the knowledge of the glory of God as the waters cover the sea" (Hab. 2:14). Many other verses attest to this (Num. 14:21; Isa. 2:2, 11:9; Zech. 14:9).

So when you die, your soul will indeed go to heaven; yet ultimately, we are not destined for heaven. Heaven is coming to earth.

> "Then I, John, saw the holy city, the New Jerusalem, coming down to earth out of Heaven from God. Behold, the tabernacle of God is with man, and He will dwell with them." Rev. 21:3

Note the motion in this verse, the direction of the energy. It does not say the tabernacle of man is with God, or that we will dwell with Him. Rather, the tabernacle of God is with man and *He will dwell with us*.

He is coming here. That's the whole point. Joining heaven and earth has always been His plan, as Ephesians 1:9-10 make clear: "He might gather together in one all things which are in heaven and earth" *This places great, if not equal value, on earth.* When this finally sinks in, it causes us to think very differently about our time on earth and our stewardship of the planet.

Look again at the verse in Revelation, it says, "The seventh angel sounded and there were loud voices in Heaven saying the kingdoms of this world have become the kingdoms of our Lord and His Christ, and He shall reign forever" (Rev. 11:15). The world *becomes* the kingdoms of Christ. So while the church has been quick to abandon planet earth as irrelevant compared to our supposed ethereal, spiritualized future, God remains fully committed to the earth.

Earth matters. Right here, right now, but also into our eternal future.

Co-Heirs

Jesus is inheriting "all things" (Heb. 1:2), including, "the nations" and the "ends of the earth" (Ps. 2:8). We get it. But why would Jesus bring along the saints?

It is staggering to realize that while Christ is *the* king, He is also called the King *of kings* (1 Tim. 6:15, Rev. 19:16). This title isn't limited to His eventual rulership over earthly potentates. He's the capital 'K'ing of little 'k'ings. Scripture goes to great pains to make sure we know who that refers to: Not Queen Elizabeth of England. Not the Tzars of Russia. Not the Emperors of China. Not the President of the United States. Not rulers of nations.

It's *us*. The faithful, blood-bought saints of God are the ones who are promised to rule and reign over planet earth as *priests* and *kings*. Jesus is *our* king by loyalty and choice, not theirs. We are the eventual kings of the universe, and He will be King of kings. There are a score of verses supporting this point:[45]

> "You've made us kings and priests, and we shall reign on the earth" (Rev. 5:10).
>
> "Now if we are children, then we are heirs—heirs of God and co-heirs with Christ" (Rom. 8:17).
>
> "If we endure, we will reign with Him" (2 Tim. 2:12).
>
> "Blessed and holy is he who has part in the first resurrection...they will be priests of God and reign with Him a thousand years" (Rev. 20:6).

Jesus is actually sharing His rule with *us*—and we are co-heirs with Jesus in the earth and all things besides!

It is mind-boggling to consider the magnitude of this responsibility. Most Christians are preparing for the idea of heaven. But if I ask, "Are you prepared for *earth*?" most would answer, "Huh?" But in fact, it's perhaps the most important question we can ask in this life: How can we be prepared to rule with Jesus?

Jesus answered this exact question in a parable.

[45] Ps 37; Matt 5:5, 25:23; Rom 8:17, Jesus' inheritance is the earth, as co-heirs, we share in His inheritance; 2 Tim 2:12; Luke 19:13,16-17; Rev 5:10; 2:26; 3:21; 20:6; 21:7

Why the Delay? Doing Business on Earth

In Jesus' day, the Jews were expecting a messiah who would establish an earthly Kingdom along the pattern of King David. Indeed the messianic title is "Son of David." So when Jesus came as the "Lamb of God who takes away the sin of the world," (John 1:29), the Jews couldn't understand that there would be two advents, the first as the Lamb, to take away sin, and the second as the Lion, to rule.

But *why*? Why not come once and set up the kingdom then? Because, while one goal is to build a kingdom, *the primary goal is to raise up little kings and queens*. Jesus came as the "seed"[46], who would "fall to the ground and die,"[47] producing a whole crop of "sons of the Kingdom."[48] Incredibly, we are called Jesus' *brothers* (Rom. 8:29, Heb. 2:11).

The *point* of the delay in Christ's second coming—i.e., the age you are now living in—is the preparation of His co-heir kings. In Luke 19, Jesus told a parable "because they thought the kingdom of God would appear immediately" (Luke 19:11). Its purpose was to warn them in advance that He would not return right away, explain why, and tell them what to do in the meantime:

The Parable of the Minas	Interpretation
"A certain nobleman went to a far country to receive for Himself a kingdom and to return.	The nobleman is Jesus, who journeyed to a "far country"—i.e. Heaven—to receive a

[46] Gen. 3:15; Mark 4:1-9, Matt 13: 1-9, Mark 4:28
[47] John 12:24
[48] Matt. 13:28

(vs 12)	kingdom.
"And he called ten of his slaves, and gave them ten minas and said to them, 'Do business with this until I come back.'" (vs. 13)	His plan was always to return, so he gave power, resources, vision and abilities to his servants. He also gave them a simple mission: "While I'm gone, do business."

Literally, in the delay between the ages, between His first coming and His second, Jesus said, "Do business." Our mandate is not to withdraw or abandon the earth as if that will somehow keep us pure of defilement. At the first coming, the angels appeared to the shepherds in the field *as they worked*. The second coming, Jesus said, "Two would be in the field" (Luke 17:36)—i.e., *working*. The parable of the Wheat and Tares, Jesus said both would grow side-by-side. We are not worry about the weeds (evil), but *be wheat*, and grow—in skill, maturity, and godliness—side-by-side with evil. The king's explicit instructions were to flood the world system with salt and light. Let's finish the parable:

The Parable of the Minas	Interpretation
"When he returned, having received the kingdom". (vs. 15a)	Jesus' second coming.
"He then commanded these servants, to whom he had given the money, to be called to him, that he might know how much every man had gained by trading. (vs. 15b)	It is the day of reckoning. The King wants to know what you did with your time and resources. Were you fruitful and productive? *Are you ready to be a king?*

"Then came the first, saying, 'Master, your mina has earned ten minas.' And he said to him, 'Well done, good servant; because you were faithful in a very little…" (vss. 16-17)

He was faithful by multiplying that which he had been given. Our earthly life is a seemingly insignificant, "very little" thing, but what we do here determines our eternal destiny.

"'Have *authority over ten cities*.'" (vs. 17)

We become co-heirs with Christ, ruling and reigning with Him. More on this later.

The ultimate king gives ultimate authority to be productive. So what is the language He employs? No surprise, it is *business* language. Do business! Be practical. Be industrious. Be innovative, hardworking. Multiply. What are we to multiply? Multiply *whatever you have been given*. If you have love, then love. If you are a teacher, then teach. If you manage, then manage:

> **6** Having then gifts differing according to the grace that is given to us, let us use them: if prophecy, let us prophesy in proportion to our faith; **7** or ministry, let us use it in our ministering; he who teaches, in teaching; **8** he who exhorts, in exhortation; he who gives, with liberality; he who leads, with diligence; he who shows mercy, with cheerfulness. (Rom. 12:6-8, NKJV)

And in everything you do, bring God's ways.

Your Earthly Internship for Your Kingly Calling

The present age could be compared to a college internship designed to train us for our eternal job.

Remember, we are the salt—the curative—of the earth, the light of the world. That means bringing the Kingdom of God, which is the power of God and the ways of God, to the earth. But if you can't be salt and light for the brief period of your mortal life, what makes you think immortality will improve your game?

This earth is our chance. Our proving ground. Where we will become little kings and queens. Where we will leaven a corrupt world with goodness, until erroneous thinking becomes eternal thinking and wrongs become rights. Until heaven is showing up on earth.

Take chaos, bring order.

Take lies, speak truth.

Take brokenness, bring healing.

Take poverty, bring aid.

Take ignorance, add knowledge.

Take unemployment, make employees.

Take a barren field, produce a crop.

Take a problem, find a solution.

Take abuse, create sanctuary.

Take pain, release mercy.

Let's be light, be salt, be God's image astride the earth—feet on the footstool. If the world is darker than it should be, it is only because we've cultivated a theology which excuses us for allowing it!

Go ahead, build a career. Build a family. Get really good at a skill, a trade or profession. Influence a sector of society that exists in darkness. Bring light. Adopt a child. Feed the poor. Invent a cure for something. Discover a new subatomic particle. Shift an industry. Turn your business into a spiritual oasis. Artistically, make something beautiful. Infuse this temporal, immoral world with eternal perspective and virtue. Pray for the ending of abortion and sex-trafficking, but also do the business of providing compelling alternatives, such as building a successful business that can hire trafficked victims, pay and shelter them, and give them a new life. Built a "charity margin" into your profit margin and then give that money away. Be a good dad, a good mom. There are a million ways to do business.

Pick one. Start. He's coming back, and He wants to see an earth with His imprint, and greet a trained king or queen He recognizes as His own.

Isn't God's Kingdom "Not of this World?"

Naturally, all this talk of the value and importance of earth leads to a reasonable question. Why did Jesus clearly state, "My kingdom is *not* of this world?" Let's look more closely at that verse. In context, Jesus was being tried before Pontius Pilate. As Pilate questioned the Lord, he asked why the Jewish nation had turned against their supposed king. Why had that happened?

Jesus answered, "My kingdom is not of this world. If it were, my servants would fight to prevent my arrest by the Jewish leaders. But now my kingdom is from another place" (John 18:36, NIV). Notice the wording. Did you catch the timing? "*Now* ('as it is,' NASB) my kingdom is not of this world."

He didn't say never. He said *at this time*, my kingdom is not yet fully established. He came to plant a seed, Himself; and soon He will return to harvest the crop—little kings and queens.

Aren't We "Foreigners in the Earth?"

You may ask, what about scriptures that say we are "aliens and foreigners in the earth" (1 Pet. 2:11, Heb. 11:13) and that we are not of this world (John 17:16)? Many sermons have affirmed that we must learn to be "in" the world, but not "of" it. Doesn't this mean we should limit our earthly involvement in business, education, or career?

Exactly the opposite!

As we have already seen, Jesus clearly commanded, "*Do business* until I come" (Luke 19:13). Engage! Roll up your sleeves and get your hands dirty. Put your whole heart into it: "*Whatever* you do, work with *all your heart*, as working for the Lord not men" (Col 3:22-24).

The true scriptural idea is to *fully engage the world system while rejecting its primary motivators of pride, materialism, and worldly pleasures*.[49] *That* is what it means to be in the world but not of it.

In Hebrews 11, Abraham is lauded as our model because the father of our faith "was looking for the city which has foundations, whose architect and builder is God" (Heb. 11:10, NIV). Abraham regarded himself as a pilgrim, a stranger in a foreign land. So do

---

[49] Rom 12:2, John 17:15, 1 John 2:16

we do the same, and say we are just passing through, temporary residents of earth, and heaven is our home?

Not exactly.

Abraham lived in the Promised Land, which in his day was as a foreigner in a foreign land. However, *it was a land he was to later inherit.*

Like Abraham, we are *now* living in our Promised Land—earth. Today, it is as foreigners, but when Jesus returns, it will be as *heirs*. Earth has been promised to us, and soon we will inherit it.

What about the Tribulation?

What about the Book of Revelation and the intense period of trouble called the Tribulation, when various catastrophic events portray vast swathes of the human population being destroyed and earth burning with fire? Fish die. Crops die. Plagues. War. What about *that* earth? As we shall see, *the purpose of these End-Time events is not to destroy the earth but to redeem it.*

But before we go to Revelation, let's first look at the parallel description of great tribulation in Matthew 24.

> "When you see standing in the holy place 'the abomination that causes desolation,' spoken of through the prophet Daniel—let the reader understand—then let those who are in Judea flee to the mountains. Let no one on the housetop go down to take anything out of the house. Let no one in the field go back to get their cloak. How dreadful it will be in those days for pregnant women and nursing mothers! Pray that your flight will not take place in winter or on the Sabbath. For then there will be great distress, unequaled from the be-

ginning of the world until now—and never to be equaled again. If those days had not been cut short, no one would survive" (Matt. 24:15-21).

No one would survive? Distress that has never been equaled? No wonder Jesus says to pity the nursing mothers! This is panic time! What's going on? Let's break it down.

"When you see the abomination of desolation"—basically a satanic symbol in the holy temple—"let those who are in Judea flee to the mountains." As bad as it sounds, our traditional interpretation (and the emotional reaction it creates) has an immediate problem, because Jesus is talking about Jerusalem, Judea, and the temple. Clearly, this is a local issue. *It's not talking about a global phenomenon.*

Maybe there is also trouble across the rest of the globe, but you can't support global destruction and tribulation with *this* verse. That's important, because when it comes to the End-Times, we tend to make broad associations that sort of mash all the bad phrases together, instead of recognizing the order, timing and scope which various verses convey. Here, Jesus isn't even inferring a global scenario. In Matthew 24, the great tribulation is, geographically at least, a Jewish event, with Jewish signals to alert a Jewish audience of the proper course of action for when that time should finally come.

Other verses *do* describe more widespread perils. Other locations on the planet will experience trouble, but the point of this verse is Judea. That's not a small detail, because the "unequaled" "great distress" by which "no one would survive" is often presented as a global phenomenon.

The Final Conflict

What about the "Bowl Judgments" in Revelation 16 that describe locusts, plagues, boils, fire, and the earth being utterly destroyed? What about the seven seals and seven trumpets that precede the seven bowls of wrath? Go read the book from chapters 6-16. It'll make the hair on your neck stand up! Unfortunately, such deeply entrenched systems of darkness and corruption will not yield easily to the rule of Christ. There will be resistance and war. Unless God judges evil, He cannot be called a just God. But He *is* just; therefore, in His righteous hatred of evil, He is absolutely committed to eradicating evil from the planet. It is both just and necessary. For pedophiles, sex traffickers, murderers etc., it will be "time's up!" Many scriptures describe this cleansing, including many of Jesus' parables.[50]

While this may sound fearful, it has already been foreshadowed in scripture. Jesus is coming as the greater Moses to confront the false gods who keep humanity enslaved to sin, much as Israel was enslaved in Egypt. Just as the ten plagues unleashed terror on a corrupt nation, the Bowls of Wrath are designed to pry loose the clutching grip of a demonic pretender who still presumes to govern the affairs of men, rather than bow the knee to Christ. Moses unleashed plagues aimed at an obstinate pharaoh and his wicked army in Exodus 14. Likewise, Jesus will confront the antichrist and his armies in Revelation 19.

But the destruction is far from absolute. Israel was preserved in the midst of these terrors. A few of the early, lesser plagues oc-

[50] 2 Thes. 2:8, 2 Thes, 1:6-10, Joel 3:12-16, Isa. 13:6-11, Isa. 63:1-6, Rev. 19:15-16, Luke 19:27, Luke 20:15-16, Matt. 21:41, Matt. 22:7,Matt 25:30, Ps. 2:1-9

curred around them, but Israel remained unharmed. The latter, more severe plagues targeted Egypt alone. Israel was afforded supernatural refuge status. Similarly, in Luke 17, when Jesus compares His coming to the days of Noah, we find evil purged away by the flood, while Noah and his family were safely sheltered in the ark. And finally, righteous Lot, the nephew of Abraham, lived in a perverse generation. When judgment came, Sodom and Gomorrah burned with fire…but Lot remained. *He inherited the land.* God is telegraphing His ways to give us confidence and peace. Yes, challenging times lie ahead, but God will prevail, life will continue, and the meek will inherit the earth (Matt. 5:5).

God is coming to *destroy* evil, not preserve it. Evil has no inheritance in the earth.

> "The lawless one will be revealed, whom the Lord will consume with the breath of His mouth and destroy at the brightness of His coming." (2 Thes. 2:8).

The dreaded Bowls of *Wrath* clarify the object of God's anger, because the Bible clearly states, "God has not destined ('appointed,' KJV) us for wrath" (1 Thes. 5:9) while also describing Jesus as He who "rescues us from the coming wrath" (1 Thes. 6:10). That's good news!

At the end of the age, the elect of God are marked by the Holy Spirit. Terrors may come, but we are preserved. "Do not harm the land or the sea or the trees until we put a seal on the foreheads of the servants of our God" (Rev. 7:3).

Preserved from wrath and sealed by God. More good news!

Fire and the New Earth

Admittedly, my dissection of the Great Tribulation comes as a series of broad strokes, more designed to rattle our rusty mental cage then to build a new one. There are many details I can't address in the limited space we have. As already stated, my main goal is to poke enough holes in the trumped up mythology we have come to accept about the End-Times so that we can deflate the lies and start building a new mindset based on the hopes and truths of scripture.

Before I close this chapter on the future of earth, let me add two more pieces to the puzzle. You may have already thought about this passage:

> [7]The heavens and the earth...are reserved for fire until the Day of Judgment and perdition of ungodly men. [10]But the day of the Lord will come as a thief in the night, in which the heavens will pass away with a great noise, and the elements will melt with fervent heat; both the earth and the works that are in it will be burned up. (2 Peter 3:7,10)

It is really just an unfortunate translation. The word translated "burned up" is better translated "exposed" or "discovered." [51] Clearly from the multitude of other references to earth, the earth continues.

The other verse that makes people scratch their head is Revelation 21:1: "Then I saw a new heaven and a new earth; for the first heaven and the first earth passed away…"

---

[51] Arichea, Daniel C. ; Hatton, Howard: *A Handbook on the Letter from Jude and the Second Letter from Peter*. New York : United Bible Societies, 1993 (UBS Handbook Series; Helps for Translators), S. 156

After all the troubles described in previous passages of Revelation, we get to those two words, "passed away," and we subconsciously substitute our own proxy words, assuming the passage is telling us that earth has been destroyed and recreated. But look again. Note what happened. It says the old earth passed away. It describes a new creation. Does that sound familiar?

> "If anyone is in Christ, he's a new creation. Old things have passed away; behold, all things have become new" (2 Cor. 5:17).

When I became a Christian, I wasn't destroyed. I suspect you weren't either. Instead, I was transformed. I still had my old body, but something powerful and complete happened at a single point in time that has been unfolding ever since, over many decades. Here I am, old earth and a new creation, all at once. It is the same thing with our planet. It will be totally remade according to God's ways and image.

Reshaped, refashioned. Not destroyed.

Not some planetary supernova—poof!—while we float around in Heaven.

Obviously, if Jesus is returning as we believe, it's not to some cosmic fireball.

No, *reborn.* You are a new creation in Christ and you will one day live on the new creation of earth, where sin and sorrow are no more. In the next two chapters, I'll discuss more from the book of Revelation, including the power of the Antichrist and whether America is doomed for her sins.

For now, let's summarize:

- The earth belongs to God
- He has given it to man as responsible stewards
- He is coming back for it
- He will establish his throne on earth forever.
- The faithful saints will reign on the earth with him, forever
- Heaven is coming to earth
- The purpose of global, concerted prayer is to bring heaven to earth

Earth has a great future. It is the seat of Jesus' eternal throne, and our home with Him. It will become His Kingdom, and be joined with heaven. Earth is not the doomed Titanic, and if today you find yourself in the lifeboat line waiting for rescue—quick!—turn around right now, make a plan, and get productive. Do business. It's *your* earth, and *your* future. Make it count.

But even if the earth itself has a future, doesn't justice demand that God punish our nations for their evil? Take America, for example, with her corrupt political agendas and her immorality. Mustn't God judge her for her sins?

CHAPTER 6

Reason #6

THERE IS HOPE FOR AMERICA

Fact:
"For the sake of ten, I will not destroy."
(Gen. 18:32, NIV)

I have a confession to make.

I love America.

I love the good I see in her: her history, her people, her entrepreneurialism, her innovation, her creativity, her openness, her generosity; I pray for her often; sometimes with the words of this famous little song:

God bless America, Land that I love
Stand beside her, and guide her
Through the night with the light from above

But while I see her good, I also see the other. Doesn't it seem sometimes like America and the western world at large have lost their moral bearings and are turning away from God and godliness in every way and as rapidly as possible?

The sin and secularization of the West and America in particular has led hundreds of Christian leaders—many eminent and highly respected—to call for God's judgment. Yet there is abundant reason to hope for the West and for America. Again, *there is a bigger picture and a better narrative that has been overlooked.*

If you are not American, I thank you for indulging me and forgiving my effusiveness! If you can bear with me, I think you will find much of it applies to you and your nation as well.

The Call for Judgment

The late, great evangelist, David Wilkerson, famous for bringing revival among the gangs of New York City, wrote *A Final Warning to America* in 1991. In that book, now twenty-five years old, Wilkerson declared unequivocally that we were about to witness the end of the United States as a world power. A new dark age was coming. His prediction was extreme and clearly wrong, but he is not alone in his view that judgment is near.

Franklin Graham, the respected son of Billy Graham, has gone on record saying, "On the issue of homosexuality and gay marriage many Americans and their political leaders are turning their backs on God. As a result, God will judge this nation for refusal to obey His Word."[52]

---

[52] CNS News, March 2014

Respected pastor and author Dr. John MacArthur has commented on President Obama's support for homosexual marriage,

> "I'd go so far as to say that what America is experiencing now is divine judgment. You ask me why I say that and I say because of Romans 1. It says 'The wrath of God is being revealed from heaven against all the godlessness and wickedness of people, who suppress the truth by their unrighteousness.' If there has ever been a nation that has suppressed the truth in unrighteousness, it's America. We have had the truth, we've had the Gospel truth, and we're founded on that. There's a Judeo-Christian approach to law, life, and social behavior. The Gospel flourished in America, but we've suppressed it at this point, so (now) the judgment of God falls."[53]

Jonathan Cahn, author of the runaway bestseller, *The Harbinger*, recently spoke at the National Day of Prayer in Washington, D.C., where he gave a dire warning of impending judgment on our nation. Part of his talk described how God has been driven out of the public square. He also mentioned abortion as he called for America to repent. His message, which resounds with millions of Christians, is one of almost inevitable judgment since at this point it is deemed necessary—for God's honor and commitment to His own holy standard—to purge America and thus halt the reign of evil. God's righteousness demands judgment.

One of my favorite speakers once put it this way: "If God doesn't judge America, He'll have to apologize to Sodom and Gomorrah." At the time, I remember grimly thinking how rightly

---

[53] Transcript excerpted from a Q&A with John MacArthur at Castle View Baptist Church, Indianapolis, Indiana: the-end-time.blogspot.com/2012/06/is-america-under-judgment.html

he had assessed the situation! You've probably heard that line. Maybe you even feel the same way.

But we've forgotten something.

Mercy and Judgment

In the days of Abraham, described in the period of scripture we now define as the "Old Covenant," the Bible reveals that Sodom and Gomorrah would have been spared for the sake of only *ten* righteous people. Ten could have spared either city! Sadly, not even so few were found, which points to the terrible level of iniquity that must have prevailed inside those walls. Yet in principle, a tiny, believing minority can beneficially intervene on behalf of a much greater population. Neither a majority, nor unanimity, are required, but only a small, believing minority.

When nine US Supreme Court justices legalized gay marriage, the call for judgment was renewed.[54] But what about God's mercy? Though Sodom and Gomorrah would have been spared for 10 righteous, apparently America's 320 million citizens are doomed for the actions of 9 unelected judges? Does God not know I live in a democracy with other people? Or that these judges were not elected by me or anyone else?

God is *merciful*. Not only is God merciful, but we live in the Age of Grace, not Law. Yes, God is timeless; He never changes. He is one hundred percent *righteous*, one hundred percent *love*, one hundred percent *just*, and one hundred percent *merciful*. We

[54] cnsnews.com/blog/michael-w-chapman/rev-graham-gay-marriage-ruling-i-pray-god-will-spare-america-his-judgment; www.wnd.com/2015/06/i-fear-judgment-befalling-america/

can't process that kind of math. We achieve balance only through mixture, only by trading one virtue for another as needed. Compared to His infinite perfections, our behavior, speech and thoughts are compromised every day, while He remains totally unblemished.

The point is this: there is a gap between our ways and God's. In this discrepancy, we don't think like Him. So when we call for judgment, we should pause and consider the difference between our logic and the divine value system, especially when the Holy Spirit clarifies the priorities of the Father with one simple statement: "Mercy triumphs over judgment" (James 2:13).

Though Sodom and Gomorrah would have been spared for 10 righteous, apparently America is doomed for the actions of 9 unelected judges?

In many respects, I think our inversion of this statement is one of the most tolerated, deeply entrenched and theologically justified sins in the church today. Simply put, we don't agree, at least not when it comes to the moral offenses of others. Oh, we'll say we agree when *we need mercy*. We'll even quote this verse. But stack up enough sins deserving of judgment in others, or in a nation, and all bets are off. So while we might agree that homosexuality, abortion and divorce are evil, and even worthy of judgment, that is very different than proclaiming that God is ready to judge, must judge, wants to judge, or *will* judge. The reason is simple. While His judgment is coming, His favor is here.

The Year of God's Favor

Jesus understood our tendency to veer off course on the topic of judgment. So in Luke 4, He launched His ministry by picking up the scroll of Isaiah and reading this:

> The Spirit of the Lord is upon me, because the Lord has anointed me to preach the gospel to the poor, to heal the brokenhearted, proclaim liberty to the captives, recovery of sight to the blind, to set at liberty those who are oppressed, to proclaim the favorable year of the Lord. (Luke 4:1-2)

He then sat down and unequivocally informed the law-abiding elders of the synagogue, "Today, this is fulfilled in your hearing."

Silence. Pin drop. Can you imagine the shock of that moment? Fulfilled? Yet the drama only heightens when we realize that Jesus intentionally left out the final key phrase, for Isaiah 61 not only promises that the Messiah will bring "a year of favor" but also a "day of the vengeance of our God" (v. 2).

Jesus said precisely what He meant to say, but what He did *not* say should ring even louder in our ears. Those two phrases describe two distinct periods of time. The age of His first coming is the age of the Lord's unmerited favor, which is where we are *right now*. We are living in the comma, the gap between those two phrases. By contrast, while the day of vengeance is coming, it's not today. In this age, mercy extends to all. The year of favor is an open invitation to everyone, regardless of race, creed or failure. Receive favor! Receive mercy!

The richness of that word, "favor," should directly challenge our thinking. The "year of *favor,*" is the year when God extends his favor to everyone. This word "favor" is rich in meaning. It means "to receive, to accept, to welcome, to be pleasing to, to extend hospitality, to take with the hand, to not refuse friendship, to receive favorably, to embrace, to make one's own, to approve, to not reject." Has God rejected America for her sins? No, because favor means to *not* reject!

Favor is not only the way God acts toward us, but is also to be the mode of our interaction with others. We, too, must make the most of every opportunity to extend hospitality, act with confidence, encourage towards godliness, approve and not reject. Don't look for doom, look for hope! Dispensationalism properly recognizes that there *is* a day of vengeance. It's coming. For those who refuse to be ruled and reigned over by Christ, the final option will, at long last, be put into play. When that moment arrives, the year of favor will end and the day of vengeance will begin. But oh how quickly we jump to conclusions and start shouting, "Judgment! Judgment!" while the year of favor still persists.

Furthermore, notice the scale of time. A day is extremely brief compared to a year. In other words, favor covers the long haul of history. Let me say it another way. God's *main relational strategy is not judgment*. He's not tapping His fingers impatiently waiting for us to get our act together, ready to bring the hammer down when the nice guy routine finally fails. That's not how He thinks or what He wants.

The Wrong Spirit

Like us, the early disciples didn't understand this part of the Lord. Much like us, they expected the Messiah to operate from a very different playbook. Surely the eschatological ruler of history would enter every town and clean house, punish evil, and overthrow resistance by any means necessary!

Then came the day Jesus entered a Samaritan village, which promptly rejected Him—darn Samaritans!—leaving two of the disciples so incensed, so outraged, that they were ready to help Jesus bring down the hammer. (I wonder if they excused their feelings as "righteous indignation," like we do today?). James and John cried out for judgment.

> "'Lord, do You want us to command fire to come down from heaven and consume them?' But He turned and rebuked them, and said, 'You do not know what kind of spirit you are of, for the Son of Man did not come to destroy men's lives, but to save them.' And they went on to another village." (Luke 9:54-56)

Ouch! When we cry out for judgment, what spirit are *we* of? If He wanted to destroy humanity, He's certainly had plenty of reason and opportunity before now, right? He could have justifiably done it in the days of Nimrod, Pharaoh, Nero, Caligula, Tamerlane, Leopold II, Attila the Hun, Genghis Khan, Robespierre, Hitler, Stalin, Mao Zedong, Pol Pot…but He didn't. Why? Because, contrary to the many voices stating otherwise, the Bible specifically says He's *not* looking for ways to destroy humanity in this age. Jesus said, "God did not send his Son into the world to *condemn* the world, but to *save* the world" (John 3:17).

Natural Disasters Don't Equate To Divine Judgment

A subset of our wrong thinking is the tendency to view natural calamity as *specifically meted out divine judgment* on sin. Oh, my friends, tread carefully here! In Jesus's own words, it is clear that we should either be silent (Matt. 7:1-3), or at minimum, extremely cautious in our readiness to judge others by ascribing causality to their misfortune. The latter warning comes from Luke 13, where Jesus corrected an erroneous tendency of the Jews to interpret local tragedies through the lens of blame and judgment. While we don't have a lot of detail on the pair of first century events He referenced, apparently 1) a group of Galilean's who were worshipping God were subsequently killed by King Herod; and 2) a tower collapsed in the city of Siloam, killing eighteen people.

> Jesus totally dismantled the idea that atrocity or disaster was the judgment of God

First century Jews exhibited a mindset much like most Christians, viewing disasters as direct, divine retribution for personal sin, i.e. when we said Hurricane Katrina leveled New Orleans because of the city's wickedness; or if the San Andreas fault blows, it's because liberal California has it coming; that sort of thing. Our blame-assigning psychological glitch dates all the way back to Adam in the garden, but also the days of Job. Don't miss what I just said there: *our need to blame somebody for something is a product of sinful thinking, not righteous thinking.* With Job, you have an innocent, righteous guy getting absolutely hammered by life, yet all his three friends can do is cast aspersions and accusations. Their assumptions boiled down to this simple formula: *God is just, therefore suffering proves guilt.*

Jesus completely dispelled this view.

> Jesus said to them, 'Do you suppose that these Galileans were greater sinners than all other Galileans because they suffered this fate...(or) that those eighteen on whom the tower in Siloam fell and killed them were worse culprits than all the men who live in Jerusalem? I tell you, no, but unless you repent, you will all likewise perish.' (Luke 13:2-5)

In the first example, which was an apparently random murder, King Herod ordered the killing. In the second, some natural disaster (possibly an earthquake) caused a stone tower to collapse, costing eighteen people their lives.

In His response, *Jesus totally dismantled the idea that atrocity or disaster was the judgment of God.* Instead of serving as valid signs of judgment, Jesus describes tragedy and calamity as simple, direct invitations to get right with God. Humans have a great need to extract meaning from tragedy, which often leads to blame. But in a fallen world, unjust, random, unpredictable things may happen at *any* time, to *any* group, for *any* reason. The only meaning to extract is that life can be unfairly cut short, so don't wait, and don't presume on the time you are given. Come to God now, because you may not have another chance. Also implied, is that if you do repent, you will not perish, because God will protect and preserve you!

It's powerful, practical and hopeful, but *not* condemning.

Why America?

The other question I have is why America? I don't understand, *why is America singled out for God's judgment*? I don't hear the same leaders calling for God's judgment on the Muslim nations, or Russia, or China or North Korea. Is America more sinful than all the other nations?

Looking back in history, it is simply not possible to conclude that American society or government is more evil today than the government of, say, the Roman Empire under Caesars Nero, Caligula or Tiberius; or that our society is more vile than that of places of the past like Egypt, Sodom and Pompeii. Actually, I must intentionally trim the length and detail of this portion, because there are so many vile periods to choose from, ranging from the unchecked appetites (including bestiality) carved into the stone of the Temples of Khajuraho in India, to the shocking deviancy and cruelty among the ancient emperors of China.

If you dare, study the extreme sensuality and sexualization of Roman culture, exemplified in a city like Pompeii, which was famously buried under a lava flow following the sudden eruption of Mount Vesuvius in 79 AD. The sudden manner of Pompeii's destruction almost perfectly preserved the ruins from decay, permitting modern archaeologists to uncover many fascinating and disturbing proclivities of the city, such as brothels seemingly on every corner and explicit pornography all over the public walls. Depraved stuff, but relatively normal for the day.

Similarly, the Roman court under Nero was a moral cesspool. I'll talk about him more later—but there was rampant corruption, depravity, incest, bribery, extortion, murder, lasciviousness. Tiberius openly practiced pedophilia. If we try to maintain that America is worse than Rome, I'm sorry, but we simply haven't fully assembled the facts. My point is that gross iniquity has dominated and defined various regions and cultures for decades and centuries at a time. In spite of her sins, the Roman Empire survived intact for 700 years (1700 years if you count the Eastern Roman Empire).

Or looking at nations in the modern era, neither can I find any reason why America is singled out for judgment. Consider:

China. Modern China is one of the most murderous nations *in human history*. It is also one of the greatest persecutors of Christians in the 20th century. This atheistic regime slaughtered 35 million of its citizens between 1949 and 1987, but that number pales in comparison to China's record on abortion. Since the Communist Party began enforcing a draconian "One Child" policy in the early 1980's, China has effectively wiped out a population *equivalent to the entire population of America*: 330 million abortions. This is nearly 13 times the rate of the United States and five times the abortion rate per capita. So, why is God singling out America rather than China?

Russia. One of the most oppressive and brutal regimes in recent history, Russia murdered 60 million of its citizens in cold blood simply because they were deemed political enemies. In addition, Russia imprisoned and/or exiled some 25 million more, including sending them to brutal slave labor. So is God really angrier at America than Russia?

Muslim nations. If you want a case study in the repression of truth, visit any number of Islamic states, some of which are the leading sponsors of global terrorism today. By modern standards, these societies are practically medieval. Women are treated like chattel, suspected criminals are given no due process, punishments are extreme, and free speech, free thought, and freedom of religion are all punishable offenses. These nations, and the extremist subcultures they foster, are beheading people on international media with no remorse. Is God more upset at America than radical Islamic societies?

We have this notion that God plays by our rules, and thinks our thoughts. But lest we think we can force God's sovereign hand with our own sense of justice, perhaps we should first explain why God gave Russia and the Muslim Arab nations much of the world's oil? Why in His infinite justice did He empower them to be so blessed? According to the above summary, they certainly don't *deserve* it.

Let's turn from nations in general to specific crimes, where further discrepancies in the national moral quotient become clear. Though many categories of data could be employed, I'll illustrate with one of the most heinous vices: sex trafficking. According to Havascope.com, publisher of *Prostitution: Prices and Statistics of the Global Sex Trade,* China (again) leads the world in money spent on prostitution, spending a staggering $73 billion annually. After China, Spain and Japan spend $26.5 and $24 billion, respectively, compared to $14 billion in the U.S. Yes, fourteen billion is tragic, but Spain and Japan have much smaller populations relative to the U.S., meaning prostitution is a disproportionately larger national sin in those nations—almost seven times greater in Spain and almost three times greater in Japan. Meanwhile, Germany's $18 billion prostitution empire is a legal industry! Is God madder at America than these nations?

How about India? According to the 2013 Global Slavery Index, almost half of the 30 million "modern slaves" in the world are from India. The same report states that ten countries account for 76% of the 30 million estimate, including: India, China, Pakistan, Nigeria, Ethiopia, Russia, Thailand, Democratic Republic of Congo, Myanmar and Bangladesh.

Now, understanding that nearly a third of sex traffic victims are children, consider the two paragraphs above in light of Jesus's warning not to cause children to stumble in sin. He said, "It would be better for (the perpetrators) to have a heavy millstone hung around his neck, and to be drowned in the depth of the sea" (Luke 18:6). Why is God ready to destroy America rather than India and Thailand?

Space does not permit discussions of how other nations also lead the U.S. in vices such as drug cartels, organized crime, drunkenness, money laundering, bribery, etc. My point is simple: America cannot be first on God's list for judgment.

How Does God Judge Nations?

The common answer to my question "Why America?" is that America will be judged with a harsher judgment because of her rich Christian history. America was founded by Christians and with Christian ideals. Neither can Europe escape a greater condemnation, as the very seat of Christianity for 2000 years, the author of the Reformation, the Age of Enlightenment, the Great Awakening, the modern missionary movement, and too much more to even name.

Cahn and many others have quoted the scripture: "To whom much is given, much is required" (Luke 12:48). But there is a problem with applying this verse: Jesus is describing his evaluation of individuals when they stand before him on judgment day; *He was not speaking of nations.*

It begs the question: how does God judge nations today?

In the Old Testament period the nation of Israel was often judged, but it is very problematic to draw parallels with any other nation, because Israel is absolutely unique in history. God Himself initiated a covenant with them; they were actually called "betrothed" to God (Jer. 2:1-3), thus their sin was viewed as adultery; at Mount Sinai, the *entire population* pledged themselves and future generations to God in faithful obedience, and the covenant was sealed in a blood rite. There is simply no other nation that can be compared to the nation of Israel. Thus taking scriptural references that are related to the nation of Israel and applying them to any other nation is faulty at best.

Israel aside, there were many other nations where destruction was prophesied in the Old Testament.[55] But in the New Testament, we find no such proclamations. *Zero.* Jesus had many opportunities to speak against the oppressive Roman occupation, but steadfastly refused (Matt. 22:15-21, John 19:1-11). Same with the Apostles, who ministered under the reigns of apostate emperors Caligula and Nero, but they too *never spoke against Rome.* The incredible wickedness of the Empire and its leaders I briefly described. Shouldn't the Apostles have called for judgment? Paul

[55] Some examples: the Amorites (Gen 15:16); Egypt (Ez. 29:15), Edom (Ez. 25:14, Jer. 49:16); Tyre (Amos 1:9-10, Ez. 26:3-21, Zech. 9:3-4), Babylon (Is. 1319, 14:23, 45:1), Nineveh (Nah. 1-3)

was eager to go to Rome and bear witness of Christ to the Roman elite—he had no thought about its judgment. Surely Rome, where Peter and Paul preached, was "given much" and much would be required? But in fact, the Roman Empire would continue and prosper for another 400 years (1400 in the Eastern Roman Empire).

The early church even prophesied a famine coming to the Roman world (Acts 11:27-30)—but *it too was not tied to judgment*. The church today is quick name wars, tragedies and natural disasters as divine judgment for sin; but Jesus, the Apostles, and the early church all refrained from doing so.

Is God judging nations in this age? The Parable of the Wheat and Tares (Matt. 13:24-30) gives us even more clues. Recall the good seed (Jesus) is sown in a field, and tares, or weeds are sown by the enemy. The farmer (the Father) *does not pluck up the weeds, but lets them grow*. As I have already discussed, this parable is a parable of our age, beginning at the first coming of Jesus (the seed is sown) and ending when Jesus returns (the harvest). One of the messages of this parable is that *God tolerates evil in this age*—He doesn't pluck it up—reserving judgment until Jesus returns.

To our minds this may seem incomprehensible, but it is God's way to leave challenges for us. He left enemies in the Promised Land to "teach the Children of Israel war" (Jud. 3:1-2). Since, as I described in the previous chapter, His main purpose is to train up little kings and queens who are overcomers, *He leaves us enemies to overcome*. He gives us worthy battles to fight in this age to prepare us for the next.

History too seems to indicate the same. I have studied perhaps a hundred civilizations ancient to modern, and with a few exceptions, I have not been able to correlate national sin to national judgment. Was France or Poland invaded by Hitler because they were guilty? Was medieval Europe at fault when decimated by plague? Why weren't the vile Vikings judged? Why were they allowed to prosper for 200 years, plundering churches, slaughtering defenseless monks, and generally wreaking havoc across Europe with impunity until their conversion?

There is clearly a final judgment of the nations when Jesus returns (Matt 25:32). But in this age, it doesn't seem that God wants to judge nations. I am not saying God can't or won't—but scripture and history and early Christian practice all seem to indicate He is mostly reserving judgment until the end of the age.

So how *does* God deal with the sins of a people? Let's look at one example:

The Samaritan Judgment

We already looked at Luke 9, when Jesus tried to enter the Samaritan village but was turned back. *They turned away Jesus, the son of God!* They rejected Him, even though He had done miracles there and walked their soil (John 4:1-40, Luke 17:11-17). Certainly "much was given" to the Samaritan people, and much would be required.

As we saw earlier, the disciples were in tune with this theme, and called for judgment. Jesus however, rebuked them saying, "You do not know what kind of spirit you are of, for the Son of Man did not come to destroy men's lives, but to save them" (Luke

9:55-56). But Jesus then takes His lesson one step deeper. In the next chapter, He tells the Parable of the Good Samaritan in which a Samaritan is the hero of the story, and the example of love (Luke 10:25-37)! Then He pummels them with more love, in Acts 1:8, commanding the freshly baptized disciples into Samaria, and the region experienced revival (Acts 8:1-25). Look what kind of God we have! He is so kind, so merciful, so gracious, so magnanimous, and *utterly devoid of ego*! So where does that leave America?

America the Beautiful

Does America have real problems? Yes. Does it feel like we've lost our way and are drifting from the most blessed path to a more dangerous path filled with many unwanted, natural consequences? Again, yes.

Yet as you can see below, America remains one of the most faith-filled nations on our planet. America has more believers per capita than any other large, developed nation in the world (don't forget the power of the righteous minority!). Only the Philippines, Chile, Israel and Poland were higher (not shown on chart).

A 2008 survey by the International Social Survey Programme showed 61% of Americans affirming, "I know that God really exists and I have no doubt about it."[56]

Only 3% picked the last option, "I don't believe in God."

In the same survey, 68% of Americans agreed that God is personal. Their faith was not some distant theism, but of a God who

[56] "Beliefs about God across Time and Countries" by Tom W. Smith, 2012. Analysis available at: http://www.norc.org/PDFs/Beliefs%20about%20God%20Report.docx. Summarized at: madeinamericathebook.wordpress.com/2012/05/01/still-under-god/

concerns himself with every human in an intimate, personal way. Only Chileans and Filipinos were more likely to agree. America is also the most gospel-sending nation on earth, and *the* most in history. Four times more missionaries are sent from America than from any other nation on the planet.[57]

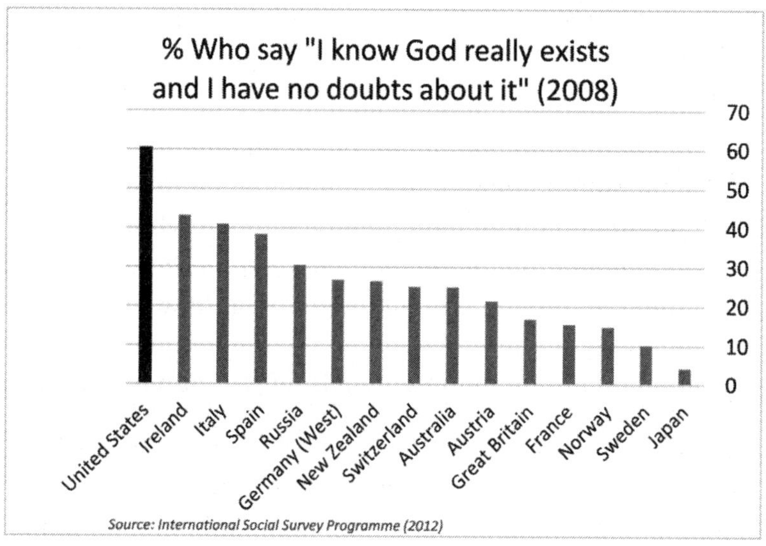

Figure 11 America, Belief in God, No Doubt

America is consistently ranked among the most generous nations on the earth. According to the 2011 World Giving Index, the United States ranked number one in the world as the most generous nation on the earth, and is the only nation to rank in the top ten in all three generosity categories:[58]

1. Helping a stranger

---

[57] "Christianity in its Global Context, 1970–2020" by The Center for the Study of Global Christianity; June 2013: www.gordonconwell.edu/resources/documents/2ChristianityinitsGlobalContext.pdf
[58] "World Giving Index 2014" by Charities Aid Foundation

2. Donating money
3. Volunteering time

Alexander Solzhenitsyn, the famous Russian novelist imprisoned in Russia for his political dissent, famously visited America and offered the keen reflections of an outsider looking in. He said, "The United States has long shown itself to be the most magnanimous, most generous country in the world."

Whenever there's a flood, an earthquake, a fire, a natural disaster, an epidemic, who's the first to help? The United States! Who helps the most, and helps most unselfishly? The United States![59] Giving USA says that Americans gave $335 billion to charity in 2013. The Lord spoke to my friend Bob Hartley once said, "America is the Good Samaritan nation." I love this description. Though the Good Samaritan had a defective religion, he had a golden heart.

America has entered international wars that were not ours, at great cost to our own sons and daughters, to rescue nations threatened by great enemies. Yes, America has had its share of despicable episodes and foolhardy exploits abroad. But America has also done great good. The words of former Secretary of State Colin Powell eloquently recall some of the positives.

> "Far from being the Great Satan, I would say that we are the Great Protector. We have sent men and women from the armed forces of the United States to other parts of the world throughout the past century to put down oppression. We defeated Fascism. We defeated Communism. We saved Europe

[59] "America the Generous" by William J. Bennett; 2011. Available at: www.cnn.com/2011/12/15/opinion/bennett-generosity

> in World War I and World War II. We were willing to do it, glad to do it. We went to Korea. We went to Vietnam. All in the interest of preserving the rights of people.
>
> "And when all those conflicts were over, what did we do? Did we stay and conquer? Did we say, 'Okay, we defeated Germany. Now Germany belongs to us? We defeated Japan, so Japan belongs to us?' No. We built them up and gave them democratic systems which they have embraced...Did we ask for any land? The only land we ever asked for was enough land to bury our dead. That is the kind of nation we are."[60]

One of America's premiere political theorists and sociologists, Seymour Martin Lipset, said, "As a nation, America is the most religious, optimistic, patriotic, rights-oriented and individualistic nation."[61] He then goes on to describe the double-edged sword of this kind of individualistic, rights-oriented culture. America has the highest crime rates, the most incarcerated population, the most lawyers per capita, along with high tort and malpractice rates, combined, unfortunately, with the lowest percentage of eligible, voting electorate. Those are sobering facts, but they are also in some sense the natural by-product of a society that has gone to great lengths to assure high levels of personal freedom.

On the other end of the spectrum, Lipset reveals that America has the highest rate of participation in voluntary organizations, the wealthiest population in terms of real income, the most productive in worker output, achieve the highest proportion of graduates or

---

[60] "MTV Global Discussion (14 February 2002)" at wikiquote.org/wiki/Colin_Powell

[61] *American Exceptionalism: A Double-Edged Sword* (New York: Norton, 1996), p. 25-26

enrollees in higher education, and continue to lead the world in upward mobility for professional and high-status occupations.

To those who are calling for the demise of America because of her sins, please stop and consider what you wish for! The developed world's most Christian nation, gone; most of world's missionaries would not exist, and many more would be sent home, unfunded; it would be a world with a fraction of today's generosity and inventions. A world without America would be a much, much darker place.

America is a flawed nation, but America is a *great* nation. In the tender mercies of God, something similar can be said of every nation. I pointed out the flaws of China, India and Russia, but I could likewise expound on their amazing contributions to human civilization over the centuries. To greater or lesser extent, every nation can lay claim to something extraordinary and unique, which is why "every tribe, tongue and nation" (Rev. 7:9) is precious enough to the Lord to be gathered around His throne one day.

A New and Better Approach

So we have this admittedly odd mix of troubles, freedom, vice, liberty, restraint, democracy, virtue, godliness and godlessness. As believers, longing for righteousness to flourish in our nation, how should we relate to America in her current state?

Let me answer by pointing to the surprising way Israel was commanded by God to relate, not to herself, but to the *despised, oppressor nation* that had conquered them. When the Jews were exiled to Babylon in 605BC, after the destruction of their beloved home, Jerusalem, God issued a terribly perplexing word through the prophet Jeremiah: "Seek *the peace and prosperity of the city to which I have carried you into exile*. Pray to the Lord for it, because if it prospers, you too will prosper" (Jer. 29:7).

The city that conquered you. Babylon. The evil city. The city that humiliated and desecrated the covenant land. Pray to the Lord for Babylon's peace. If you do, *you* will have peace.

Hundreds of years later, Paul must have seemed similarly off his rocker when he instructed other Christians in how to relate to the oppressive, wicked government of Rome.

> "Therefore I exhort first of all that supplications, prayers, intercessions, and giving of thanks be made for all men. For Kings and all who are in authority except that we may lead a quiet and peaceable life in all godliness and reverence for this is good and acceptable in the sight of God our Savior" (1 Tim. 2:1-3).

It's good and acceptable to pray for a wicked government. Worse, submit to them, pray for those leaders. Give thanks *for* them. In other words, bless your nation.

Let there be no confusion about this. Paul is telling Christians to pray for *Nero*, Caesar of Rome. Now, depending on your politics, you may despise the policies of our current president, the last president, or the next president. It doesn't matter whether our leader is a Democrat or a Republican, he or she is *not* Nero. Nero murdered his mother and brother, then married his step-sister. Historians tell us that he had Christians sewn up in animal skins and fed them to the dogs. He coated them in wax, tied them to trees and lit them afire as human torches. He beheaded Paul and crucified Peter. This was Nero.

God, bring judgment! Rome is wicked. Caesar is wicked! No, no…pray for the king.

Should we rage against our nation? Curse it? No, pray *for* it.

Then do more. Be even bolder. *Bless*!

Do more still. *Build* something better, *show* something truer, *reveal* something more beautiful. Whatever failure, whatever vice causes you to grieve, bring to it the light of Christ. Demonstrate the better kingdom and the ways of a better king. Let love and mercy triumph over judgment. Let us not view America as doomed and judged, but as residing in the window of favor, ripe for transformation.

Unashamedly, I say, *God bless America*. And God bless every other nation on earth as well.

CHAPTER 7

Reason #7

THE END OF THE AGE IS NOT TROUBLING

Fact:
"You will hear of wars and rumors of wars. See that you are not troubled; for all these things must come to pass..."
(Matt. 25:6)

This is a big chapter, because the End-Times are a big fear. Most End-Times books and teachings leave people utterly terrified. They overstate the negatives and underreport the positives. The average believer is left in the lurch, since fear is produced rather than faith.

But when Jesus gave His discourse on the End Times, He wanted to make sure that didn't happen! He is the good shepherd, wise and kind. He emphasized this main point right at the beginning: "*Do not be troubled.*" The End-Times were *not something to be feared*, Jesus said:

> [6] And you will hear of wars and rumors of wars. See that you are not troubled; for all these things must come to pass. (Matt 24:6)

This chapter is for those who have looked at the End Times and found themselves troubled. If this is not you, feel free to jump to the next chapter. As I mentioned earlier, space does not permit me to set forth a systematic study of the End Times here; my goal is not to try to answer every question or to un-puzzle every passage, but simply to point out a few of the misplaced fears in some of the commonly held End-Times views.

By now you may be wondering what exactly I believe about the End-Times. I have purposely avoided directly debating eschatological models to this point, because my goal in this book is not to convince you of my personal End-Times views, but to simply root out any hopelessness and pessimism in your own views. But plainly, here are my views: As I said before, I'm a Bible-believing literalist, a confessing, conservative Evangelical, committed to the infallibility of scripture; I am fully convinced that Jesus will literally, physically return to earth; my roots and core convictions largely bend toward what some call "Apostolic Premillennialism,"[62] with a few differences.[63] While I'm more convinced than

[62] "Apostolic Premillennialism" is distinguished from "Historic Premillennialism" merely by the addition of a victorious, rather than defeated church at the end of the age. A much greater distinction exists between Historic/Apostolic Premillennialism and its Darbyist subset, "Dispensational Premillennialism." Core attributes of Apostolic Premillennialism involve 1) a literal, chronological hermeneutic for most of the book of Revelation, including a personal Antichrist, one-world government, rebuilt Jerusalem temple, and physical mark of the beast; 2) separate, but ultimately conjoined purpose for Israel and the Church (not "Replacement Theology"), 3) rejection of a pre-tribulation rapture event; 4) the largest evangelism harvest in history; 5) the earthly millennial reign of Jesus for one thousand years following His return.

[63] I see high exegetical merit in a partial preterist view; I am not sure there must be a second temple; and while most expect a revival resembling that of Finney or Wesley, I am convinced the next harvest will look more like the Age of Enlighten-

I've ever been, I'm also less dogmatic than I've ever been. I've come to appreciate how each of the main eschatological models can legitimately claim some measure of support from both scripture and key leaders throughout history.

For those who are Premillennial, the next two chapters will address a few of the main ideas that cause fear. First, let's tackle Jesus' great End-Times discourse (Matt. 24, Luke 21, Mark 13), which has caused much consternation amongst believers.

Jesus Talks End-Times

They were speaking of Herod's Temple and how it was beautifully adorned, and then Jesus drops a verbal bomb. "These things which you see (i.e., the Temple)—the days will come in which not one stone shall be left upon another that shall not be thrown down." (Luke 21:5-6).

Let me tell you, that got their attention! The Temple was the sacred center of Jewish life. They considered it the navel of the earth, the center of creation, the locus of God's presence. Privately, they ask for more insight: "Teacher, but when will these things be? And what sign will there be when these things are about to take place?"

Jesus answers their question, which, in context, clearly relates to when the temple they were looking at—Herod's temple—would be destroyed and its stones cast down, not about the end of the age (more on this later):

---

ment. In my book *Marketplace Christianity*, I pointed out that 97% of Christians are not called to full-time vocational ministry. They are the "Great Army" of God who are now being awakened and activated for the next great move of God, one which will transform every sphere of life (a Second Age of Enlightenment) as well as bring in a great harvest of souls.

> [8] And He said: "Take heed that you not be deceived. For many will come in My name, saying, 'I am He,' and, 'The time has drawn near.' Therefore do not go after them. [9] But when you hear of wars and commotions, do not be terrified; for these things must come to pass first, but the end will not come immediately."
>
> [10] Then He said to them, "Nation will rise against nation, and kingdom against kingdom. [11] And there will be great earthquakes in various places, and famines and pestilences; and there will be fearful sights and great signs from heaven. (Luke 21:8-11, NKJV)

Most Bible readers automatically assume these things must be in the future, because they are not well-versed in history. But these events were fulfilled in the 40-year span between when Jesus spoke them and the destruction of the temple in 70 AD:

- False Christs. At least five "false Christs" arose in that brief 40-year span, claiming to be messiah and deceiving many.
- Wars and commotions. As recounted by the historian Josephus, the region of Judea was almost perpetually troubled with wars and commotions. Continual bloodshed occurred in the 40 year gap between Jesus's death and the destruction of the temple in Jerusalem in 70 AD.
- Earthquakes. At least nine major earthquakes were recorded in the wider Mediterranean region, including huge tremors that destroyed Laodicea, Colossae, and Hierapolis.
- Famines and Pestilences (disease). A major famine spread throughout the Roman world during the reign of Claudius,

along with major pestilences that devastated Babylon in 40 AD, and Rome in 65 AD.

- Fearful sights and great signs from heaven. A comet appeared in the sky in 66 AD, just prior to the beginning of the Roman onslaught in Judea. It would have been a fearful sign indeed, as comets were considered by the ancients as messengers of doom.

Then Jesus continues, warning them that before any of these things, a great persecution would arise:

> [12] But before all these things, they will lay their hands on you
> and persecute you, delivering you up to the synagogues and
> prisons. You will be brought before kings and rulers for My
> name's sake. [13] But it will turn out for you as an occasion for
> testimony. [14] Therefore settle it in your hearts not to meditate
> beforehand on what you will answer; [15] for I will give you a
> mouth and wisdom which all your adversaries will not be able
> to contradict or resist. [16] You will be betrayed even by parents
> and brothers, relatives and friends; and they will put some of
> you to death. [17] And you will be hated by all for My name's
> sake. [18] But not a hair of your head shall be lost. [19] By your pa-
> tience possess your souls. (Luke 21:12-19, NKJV)

This terrible persecution took place after the death of Jesus and throughout the next forty years. Its early years were documented in the book of Acts:

They will deliver you to synagogues. Saul persecuted believers (Acts 9:2; 22:19, 26:11); Paul was flogged by the Jews (2 Cor. 11:24).

Thrown in prison. Peter and the Apostles were imprisoned (Acts 5:19- 25); Saul threw many in prison (Acts 8:3, 22:4, 26:10); Herod imprisons Peter (Acts 12:4–6); Paul and Silas were imprisoned (Acts 16:16–40).

You will be brought before kings. Peter was brought before Herod (Acts 12:1–11); Paul before Agrippa (25:13–26:32), Peter and Paul before Nero.

And rulers: Paul was brought before Felix (Acts 23:24–24:27); Paul before Festus (25:1–26:32).

Persecution of Christians reached epic proportions in 64 AD when Emperor Nero laid blame on Christians for the fire that destroyed three-fourths of Rome. Persecution of Christians became public policy across the Empire; they were slain in gladiatorial games, flayed alive, and used as human torches.

The Destruction of Jerusalem

All these things were just precursors, signs, that would precede the final act—the destruction of Jerusalem, as the disciples had asked about. Jesus then described the coming destruction:

> [20] "But when you see Jerusalem surrounded by armies, then know that its desolation is near. [21] Then let those who are in Judea flee to the mountains, let those who are in the midst of her depart, and let not those who are in the country enter her. [22] For these are the days of vengeance, that all things which are written may be fulfilled. [23] But woe to those who are pregnant and to those who are nursing babies in those days! For there will be great distress in the land and wrath upon this people. [24] And they will fall by the edge of the

> sword, and be led away captive into all nations. And Jerusalem will be trampled by Gentiles until the times of the Gentiles are fulfilled. (Luke 21:20-24, NKJV)

Jesus *precisely detailed* the sequence of events that befell the holy city. Around 60 AD skirmishes began to break out between the Jews and the Romans. In 66 AD, the Romans retaliated by plundering the temple and slaughtering 6,000 Jews, igniting a full-scale revolt.

The Roman military commanded by Cestius Gallus marched with 30,000 soldiers to Jerusalem to put down the rebellion. They subdued the countryside—Acre, Caesarea, Jaffa, Lydda—slaughtering as they went, then surrounded Jerusalem and began a siege. For unknown reasons, they suddenly withdrew, then were ambushed and crushed by the Jews, in one of the worst defeats of the Roman Empire in history. Romans were shocked. They would of course respond with overwhelming force to subjugate the rebellious province once and for all.

Emperor Nero dispatched general Vespasian and 60,000 troops (67 AD) to punish the rebellion. By 68 AD northern Israel was crushed, and he began cleansing the coastline, then finally turned to the Jordan valley, subduing it. Most of Israel was razed, and some 100,000 Jews were killed or sold into slavery in this campaign. Subdued on three sides, he now moved his armies just outside Jerusalem. As he was preparing for the final assault, news reached him that Nero had committed suicide. He withdrew his troops and returned to Rome where he became emperor. Once again the city was spared.

The third siege would not end the same.

Vespasian's son Titus assumed command of the legions and immediately pushed toward Jerusalem, driving a tidal wave of refugees before him, most of whom took shelter in the heavily fortified city. He besieged Jerusalem just as Passover began, almost precisely 37 years from Jesus' crucifixion. Josephus tells us as many as 1,000,000 Jews were packed in the city. Half were pilgrims, now trapped in the city and living in tents. In fierce fighting, and with heavy losses, the Romans breached two of the three city walls. But upon hearing of food shortages inside the city, Titus decided to let starvation and disease do his work.

The Romans then encircled the city with a wall five miles long and waited. In an act of pure fanaticism, the Jewish zealots inside burned the city's store of grain to force the defenders to fight instead of negotiate! Many starving citizens attempted escape but were trapped by the Roman wall. They were crucified facing toward Jerusalem, 500 per day, nailed in different postures for the amusement of the soldiers. Because it was believed the Jews swallowed their gold to preserve it, many were eviscerated by their captors. The death rate accelerated—according to one defector, 115,880 bodies were thrown into the Valleys of Hinnom[64] and Kidron.

Weakened by months of starvation and infighting by the Jews, the city was captured and razed, and the inhabitants slaughtered. The precious temple was burned and destroyed. Josephus tells us 1.1 million Jews were slaughtered, and another 97,000 enslaved.

---

[64] This is the same valley Jesus made reference to in describing hell, "the Gehenna of Hell" (Matt. 5:22, 29-30, etc.)

> And they will fall by the edge of the sword, and be led away captive into all nations. (vs. 24a)

Approximately *one-third* of the entire Jewish race perished.

According to Roman writer Philostratus, Titus refused to accept a wreath of victory, saying he was "merely the instrument of the wrath of God."

> For there will be great distress in the land and wrath upon this people. (vs. 23)

Amazingly, no Christians perished. According to historian Eusebius, "The whole body of the church of Jerusalem, having been commanded by a divine revelation before the war, removed from the city, and dwelt at a certain town beyond the Jordan, called Pella."[65] In the mercy of God, they had Jesus' red-letter prediction, a recent divine revelation of warning, and not one, but two chances to depart the city when the armies surrounding it withdrew.[66] The Christians departed the city after the lifting of Cestius Gallus' first siege in 66 AD. And Pella is in a region of rugged mountains, as just Jesus instructed!

My friends, these are the plain facts of history, and they happened *exactly* as Jesus promised. These events transpired during the specific timeframe of the temple's destruction. It was truly the beginning of sorrows.

But as bad as it was, far worse was yet in store.

---

[65] Eusebius, *Ecclesiastical History*, 3:5:3

[66] The lifting of the first siege of Jerusalem by Cestius Gallus in November of 66 AD; and the withdrawal of Vespasian's army in July 69 AD.

The Final Jewish War

The third and final Jewish revolt began 62 years later. In 132 AD, Emperor Hadrian began the construction of a new city, dedicated to Jupiter, on the ruins of Jerusalem. It was to be a Roman city, with a grand temple to Jupiter built atop the ruins of the Jewish temple. He forbade circumcision, which had offended Roman sensitivities for some time. It was the most sacred rite in Judaism, the very identity of a Jew. Judaism itself was being trampled, and the results were predictable: "The whole of Judea had been stirred up…Jews everywhere were showing signs of disturbance, were gathering together, and giving evidence of great hostility to the Romans."[67]

A new leader, Simon bar Kokhba, was hailed as the Messiah, and initiated a revolt. In the first battle they badly defeated the outnumbered Romans. The Romans made several more attacks and were soundly defeated. The Jews were convinced that this was the war of the Apocalypse as prophesied by Daniel and Zechariah, which the victories seemed to confirm.

In response, Hadrian amassed one of the largest Roman armies ever deployed—fully one third of the entire army—with elements of 12 legions, and summoned his top general Severus, from Britain.

The carnage was unparalleled.

> [Severus] was able, rather slowly, to be sure, but with comparatively little danger, to crush, exhaust and exterminate

[67] Cassius Dio (Roman historian), *Roman History*, 69.12.1-2

> them. Very few Jews in fact survived. Fifty of their most important outposts [fortified towns] and 985 better known villages were razed to the ground. 580,000 were killed in the various engagements or battles. As for the numbers who perished from starvation, disease or fire, that was past finding out. Thus nearly the whole of Judaea was made desolate. (Cassius Dio, Roman history 69.13.2-3)

Incredibly, according to Jewish tradition, the last fortress fell on the 9th of Av, 136 AD, exactly 66 years from the date of the destruction of Herod's Temple and 721 years from the destruction of Solomon's Temple. It was a massacre—according to the Talmud, 800,000 were slaughtered in this final battle alone. The Romans "went on killing until their horses were submerged in blood to their nostrils." Following the final battle, the Roman legions went on a rampage of systematic killing, eliminating all remaining Jewish villages in the region and seeking out the refugees.

Historians tell us *half to two-thirds* of the Jewish race were killed, and as much as *90% of the region of Judea.*[68]

Those who weren't killed were sold into slavery, the total number of which exceeded the number killed according to one writer. There was such a glut of Jewish slaves on the market that the price of slaves fell across the Roman Empire—a slave could be purchased for the price of a horse.

Caves from this period have been discovered throughout Judea which show how the few who did escape managed to survive.[69]

---

[68] Yehoshafat Harkabi, *The Bar Kokhba Syndrome: Risk and Realism in International Politics*

I can understand if it seems I am overstating Roman brutality. Modern sensibilities cannot comprehend the ancient mindset. Rome ruled with an iron first. As long as you submitted without question to *absolute* Roman authority, Roman taxes, and conscription into the Roman army, you survived. Those who refused were mercilessly and systematically annihilated, in retribution and in warning to others. Just as an example, one Roman general told his soldiers, "Let no one escape sheer destruction, no one in our hands, not even the babe in the womb of the mother, if it be male; let it nevertheless not escape sheer destruction." It was the Roman way. It was considered good governance, the way an empire was built and maintained. Without modern technology, it was the only way for the ancients to achieve national security. God described the Roman Empire this way:

> 40 The fourth kingdom [Rome] shall be as strong as iron, inasmuch as iron breaks in pieces and shatters everything; and like iron that crushes, that kingdom will break in pieces and crush all the others. (Daniel 2:40)

Hadrian had enough of the seditious religion of Judaism, and set about to eradicate it once and for all. He prohibited the Torah law and the Hebrew calendar, and executed Judaic scholars. The sacred scroll was ceremonially burned on the Temple Mount. At the former Temple sanctuary, he installed two statues, one of Jupiter and another of himself over the site of the Holy of Holies. Over the tomb of Jesus venerated by Christians, he erected a temple to the goddess Aphrodite. Before the southern gate the Romans erect-

---

[69] "Seek the LORD, all you meek of the earth...it may be that you will be hidden (protected) in the day of the LORD's judgments" (Zeph. 2:3). "Come, my people, enter your chambers, And shut your doors behind you; Hide yourself, as it were, for a little moment, Until the indignation is past." (Isa 26:20)

ed a marble statue of a pig. In an attempt to erase any memory of Judea or Ancient Israel, he wiped the name off the map and replaced it with Syria Palaestina, after its previous inhabitants, the Philistines. He re-established Jerusalem, but now as the pagan city of Aelia Capitolina, and Jews were forbidden from entering it, except once per year.

The majority of the Jewish population of Judea was either killed, exiled, or sold into slavery after the revolt. A Jewish state would not exist for another 1800 years. It was the end of Judaism as instituted by Moses and practiced for nearly 1500 years, with feasts and temple worship at its core. The new synagogue-based Judaism had to be completely re-interpreted from the Mosaic Law.

The Times of the Gentiles

Jesus prophesied, "Jerusalem will be trampled by Gentiles until the times of the Gentiles are fulfilled" (Luke 21:24b). The Romans trampled Jerusalem, but it was just the beginning:

- In 325 AD Christian emperor Constantine tore down the temple of Jupiter and built a church.
- In 691 AD, a Muslim caliph set up the Dome of the Rock over the church. He also issued a pact known as *The Umariyya Covenant* which permitted Jews to once again live and worship inside Jerusalem for the first time in nearly 500 years.
- The Christian crusaders took the city in 1099, then lost it to Muslims again in 1187.

Since 70 AD, Jerusalem has been trampled underfoot by Gentiles in the form of Roman, Christian, or Muslim control.

Jesus' timeline has been historically precise:

1. Persecution of the saints, which would be an occasion for testimony.
2. False Christs, wars, rumors of wars, plagues, pestilences, famines and earthquakes.
3. Jerusalem surrounded by armies and destroyed, the Jewish people killed and enslaved, and Jerusalem trampled by the gentiles.
4. The "Times of the Gentiles."

How could Jesus' prediction be more exact? I gave a lot detail, so that you could compare for yourself Jesus' prophecy and historical fact. Jesus spoke His words around 30 AD. He was asked a question about the destruction of Herod's Temple, and *His answer has been one hundred percent fulfilled.* At an explicit, historical level, it's a done deal. Many agree: most Orthodox Christians, early commentators and church fathers had the view that these verses were fulfilled in 70 AD.

Not only has every facet of Jesus' timeline been fulfilled, but *how can it be fulfilled again?* It would require a new "Times of the Jews", then a new season of persecution and precursors; then Jerusalem would again have to be surrounded by armies and destroyed, followed by a second "Times of the Gentiles," followed by the return of Jesus. I simply don't see how it would be possible.

Could there really be *another* destruction of Jerusalem for which those prophecies, seemingly settled in the past, remain as a type and shadow for the future—a "then *and* now" scenario? Many God-fearing scholars fall on both sides of this question. In such a case, while one "great tribulation" has certainly already been fulfilled, many believe the events of 70 AD could be foreshadowing another, similar period of time in the future. But it begs the question: *if the most literal interpretation is settled in the past, how can we be dogmatic that there will be a future application*?

My friends, today we live in the "Times of the Gentiles," right in the middle of Jesus' timeline. Only the return of Jesus remains:

> [25] "And there will be signs in the sun, in the moon, and in the stars; and on the earth distress of nations, with perplexity, the sea and the waves roaring; [26] men's hearts failing them from fear and the expectation of those things which are coming on the earth, for the powers of the heavens will be shaken. [27] Then they will see the Son of Man coming in a cloud with power and great glory. [28] Now when these things begin to happen, look up and lift up your heads, because your redemption draws near." (Luke 21:25-28)

These verses haven't happened yet. As often happens in scriptural prophecy, we are paused between verses 24 and 25—a pause called "the Times of the Gentiles."

Understanding Matthew 24

Before we move on, let's take a quick look at the parallel passage in Matthew 24. Jesus gave a single speech which was recorded by both different writers. Each brings unique elements to light, but because they stem from the same speech, the best way to interpret them is to combine their elements. Here are some of the unique details recorded in Matthew:

The gospel preached. Before the temple is destroyed, the "gospel of the kingdom will be preached in all the world as a witness to all the nations, and then the end will come" (Matt. 24:14). The gospel of the Kingdom was, in fact, preached throughout the known world. The exact Greek word is *oikoumene*, which literally means, "the portion of the earth inhabited by the Greeks as distinguished from barbarians." The civilized, Greek-speaking world received the gospel through the tireless labors of the newly spirit-filled believers and the courage of the apostles, who, with the exception of John, were all martyred for their faith. After the scattering of the disciples, "*then* the end will come," meaning the end of the Age of the Jews, and of Jerusalem and her temple, bringing to a close one and a half millennia of Jewish temple worship.

Abomination of Desolation. In Luke's account, the sign to flee was when you saw "Jerusalem surrounded by armies," you would know "its desolation was near." In Matthew, the warning is of an "abomination of desolation," that would be the sign to flee. Note the use of the same word, *desolation*.

> [15] When you see the 'abomination of desolation,' spoken of through Daniel the prophet, standing in the holy place (let the reader understand), [16] then those who are in Judea must flee to the mountains. (Mt. 24:15-16).

When Jesus spoke this phrase around 30 AD, an "abomination of desolation" had already occurred. I've already mentioned Antioch IV Epiphanes. In 167 BC, he entered Jerusalem and dedicated the temple to Zeus. He then began sacrificing pigs, scattering the unclean blood on the sacred altar, and forbade the practice of the Jewish religion, including rites of circumcision and Sabbath-keeping. The name, "Epiphanes," means "*God manifest*." Antioch declared himself to be god and set up a statue of Zeus in the holy place of Yahweh.

Jesus references this tragic historical event with good reason. As one of the most offensive and heinous episodes in Jewish history, such a vivid word picture would sear itself in the Jewish imagination as a marker for things to come. To a Jew, the "abomination of desolation" was a clearly understood symbol—*the profaning of the Temple.*

God is so merciful, there were actually several such warnings of the coming destruction. In 40 AD Roman Emperor Caligula ordered his statue be placed in the Temple in Jerusalem. Two legions of soldiers marched to Jerusalem to complete the task, but stopped when Caligula died. The abomination of desolation did not take place, but it was a warning to pay attention.

An even clearer warning took place in Pilate's day. He installed a legion of Roman soldiers in the Antonia Fortress (on the temple mount) and they worshipped the image of Caesar their ensign every evening and every morning. Remember, Caesar was a self-proclaimed God. When the Jews saw it, they appealed to Pilate, "Kill us, if you will, but take that abomination of desolation out of our Holy City and from the neighborhood of our holy temple."[70]

A third warning appeared in 66 AD when Roman soldiers entered the temple and plundered 17 talents of gold. The temple was holy ground, and was considered profaned by the entrance of a

[70] B.H. Carroll, *An Introduction of the English Bible*, p. 263-264

gentile. That Christians departed Jerusalem at this time implies they may have seen this as the abomination of desolation.

An even more egregious profaning took place in 70 AD after Titus' army had burned and occupied the Temple, but before the city had been completely overrun. Josephus tells us the Roman soldiers "brought their ensigns to the temple and set them over against its eastern gate; and there did they offer sacrifices to them."[71] Remember, the ensigns were objects of worship and had an image of the deified Caesar. This would certainly seem to qualify.

If not, the abomination of desolation would have occurred when Hadrian placed the image of Jupiter on the temple mount in 136 AD, or when the Dome of the Rock was erected on the temple site in 691 AD to worship Allah. At one or more of these events it would certainly have to be said the abomination of desolation has been fulfilled.

<u>The Great Tribulation</u>. In Matthew, Jesus is clearly referencing the same destruction of Jerusalem and calls it the "great tribulation." He addresses the specific group of people who would be affected, "those who are in *Judea*." His words were merciful, providing advance guidance for the proper response:

> [15] "Therefore when you see the 'abomination of desolation,' spoken of by Daniel the prophet, standing in the holy place" (whoever reads, let him understand), [16] "then let those who are in Judea flee to the mountains. [17] Let him who is on the housetop not go down to take anything out of his house. [18]

[71] Josephus, *Wars of the Jews*, 6.23-24

> And let him who is in the field not go back to get his clothes. [19] But woe to those who are pregnant and to those who are nursing babies in those days! [20] And pray that your flight may not be in winter or on the Sabbath. [21] For then there will be great tribulation, such as has not been since the beginning of the world until this time, no, nor ever shall be. [22] And unless those days were shortened, no flesh would be saved; but for the elect's sake those days will be shortened. (Matt. 24:15-22)

This is extremely practical concern on the part of Jesus for the day when armies would surround Jerusalem (the location is clearly Jerusalem and Judea). *Then* you will know that a great tribulation has come. You will know to flee. I cannot think of a better phrase to describe the horrors that occurred during the Jewish-Roman wars between 66 and 136 AD.

Most Dispensationalists assume the great tribulation is a global event, but clearly it is focused on Judea alone. It is also often described as a global obliteration, but clearly they were expected to flee and survive, as the Christians did in Pella.

The word "tribulation" inspires much fear, but it simply means trials and testings. It is used 30 times in the New Testament, for example: "In the world you will have tribulation; but be of good cheer, I have overcome the world" (John 16:33). The "great tribulation" is also mentioned in Rev. 7:14 as producing martyrs. This could be a reference to the events of 70-136 AD, or it could reference another time.

Jesus made a few other statements in Matthew 24 that have been far too broadly interpreted. He describes the great tribulation as something that "has not been since the beginning of the world until this time, nor ever shall be." This in fact is quite comforting! We will never again see anything equivalent to those horrific days. He also said, "Unless those days were shortened, no flesh would be saved; but for the elect's sake those days will be shortened." The "flesh" he is talking about is Judean flesh; and the "elect" refers to both Jews (God's chosen people) and Christians. Remember that in those days the majority of the Church were converted Jews and still identified as such. They were spared by the shortening of the crisis.

I hope this helps settle things for you. We almost certainly will see wars, persecutions, earthquakes, etc. in the future. But the prophecy having been fulfilled already, none if these negatives are *Biblically required* any longer to be fulfilled. We can take a deep breath, knowing we have a wide-open future.

While in my view most of Jesus' End-Times discourse is fulfilled, many other End-Times prophecies are not. What about the Antichrist? Should we be afraid?

The Limited Power and Reach of the Antichrist

Perhaps nowhere is fear more palpable than in discussions of the one known as the Antichrist. This is because the prophetic literature inadvertently magnifies the Antichrist, and minimizes Jesus. While this is not their goal—far from it!—it is the natural consequence of their focus, just as the ten spies magnified the giants, while the two spies magnified God. Our perspective fuels our outlook. Do you see a bright, hopeful future filled with Jesus and His ways, or a dim, gloomy future filled with fear and Antichrist terror?

In general terms, the Biblical narrative is pretty well-known: there is a mark, financial restriction, along with persecution and great evil. However, explanations of these difficult passages have widely varied over the centuries, partly because the language is highly symbolic, and partly because each generation's perspective is unwittingly governed by the times in which they live, including our own. To begin with, let's acknowledge that Revelation 13 actually describes two beasts. One rises from the sea, the other from the earth. Some say the first is a kingdom, and the second is the antichrist. Others say the first is the antichrist, and the second is "the beast" or "false prophet." Similarly, some claim this has *already* occurred in history, *is* occurring, or *will* occur. Which is it?

As for timing, I tend to believe all three views are valid. While an ultimate, future embodiment is coming, a lesser measure of the "antichrist system" is currently active and has also been strongly foreshadowed in history (*vis-a-vis* Antioch Epiphanes, Nero, Hitler, et al). Again, my goal is not to do a full contextual study, parse the Greek, and otherwise bog us down in a myriad of details. Frankly, I'm not sure we'll really know the best interpretative model until it actually unfolds. Rather, I mainly want to challenge fears rooted in the popular notion that the power of the antichrist will be virtually unlimited in the near future. It's simply not true! In ideological terms, an anti-God mentality has existed in the earth since the Garden of Eden, while more specific forms of Antichrist thinking have sought traction since the time of Christ. Thus, the antichrist/kingdom/beast combination may be powerful, but it is nothing new, and God is more powerful still, as we will see.

Sheep and Goats

Revelation 13 famously describes "two beasts." One rises from the sea (v. 1) and is empowered by the dragon. The second rises from the earth (v. 11) and speaks like the dragon. To the first beast "it was granted…to wage war with the saints and to overcome them. And authority was given him over every tribe and tongue and nation" (v. 7). A few verses later, we see the second beast causing all, "both great and small, rich and poor, free and slave, to receive a mark on their right hand or on their foreheads, and that no one may buy or sell except one who has the mark or the name of the beast, and the number of his name" (v. 16-17).

In what is popularly referred to as the "mark of the beast," no one may buy or sell unless they bear this unique mark. Yet please notice, while this passage supplies us with the *rule*, it does not necessarily indicate the *practice*. Obviously, many will choose not to obey the rule. We'll come back to this surprisingly widespread resistance to the mark, but let's briefly jump ahead to Revelation 19, which describes Jesus personally returning to confront the antichrist and his armies at Jerusalem. It is a brief struggle, as Jesus utterly destroys his enemies.

> "And the beast was seized, and with him the false prophet who performed the signs in his presence, by which he deceived those who had received the mark of the beast and those who worshiped his image; these two were thrown alive into the lake of fire which burns with brimstone. And the rest were killed with the sword which came from the mouth of Him who sat on the horse, and all the birds were filled with their flesh." Rev. 19:17-21

Putting the two passages together, those who receive the anti-christ/"beast" mark also form the army of the antichrist—likely a conglomeration of military, political and social alliances—which will face the unfettered wrath of Jesus when He returns, since human loyalists to the beast are literally worshipping demons and perpetrating abominations on the earth. Thus, the culmination of history only reserves mercy for the redeemed, and for the earth itself; there is no mercy for evil in that day. Presently, Jesus bids all to believe and receive salvation. But in that day, invitations cease so that He can purge every trace of evil. Why does the Lord do this? Because He is just.

But let's untangle some of the details that tend to get lost in the broad strokes. My conviction is to compare scripture with scripture to make sure that we aren't forcing a human interpretation onto the divine storyline. In Matthew 25, which is set in this same period of time and generally referred to as "The Judgment of Christ," Jesus foretells a time when nations will be evaluated and divided into those allied to the Kingdom of God versus those loyal to the beast.

> "But when the Son of Man comes in His glory, and all the angels with Him, then He will sit on His glorious throne. All the nations will be gathered before Him; and He will separate them from one another, as the shepherd separates the sheep from the goats; and He will put the sheep on His right, and the goats on the left. Then the King will say to those on His right, 'Come, you who are blessed of My Father, inherit the kingdom prepared for you from the foundation of the world.'" Matt. 25:31-34.

Context matters. As you already know, Matthew 24 is the End-Times discourse where Jesus personally discusses events surrounding His return. Matthew 24 lays out a series of markers, like events on a timeline. The next chapter, Matthew 25, directly continues this discourse, but the presentation style shifts briefly to two parables. With these, Jesus defines the two criteria by which He will evaluate the saints when He returns: wisdom and faithfulness. The Parable of Ten Virgins describes wisdom, and the Parable of Talents describes faithfulness. However, beginning in verse 31, we shift back into non-parabolic mode where Jesus is no longer evaluating His saints, but the nations. This is "The Judgment" section. In that day, He will divide the nations into categories of "sheep nations" and "goat nations."

To reiterate, this is *not* a parable like that of the virgins and the talents. It is a definite point in history when Jesus "comes in glory and all the holy angels with him" to "sit on the throne of his glory" in Jerusalem, at which time, "nations will be gathered to him." The question arises: who are these nations who will be separated into sheep and goats? Think about it for a moment. At this stage of the second coming, the saints have already experienced resurrection, and those who took the mark of the beast have all been killed during the End-Times battles described in Revelation 19.[72] So who is being divided in Matthew 25? If you don't see the dilemma yet for traditional eschatological models, *entire nations remain on the earth* after the judgment. Thus, clearly, *entire nations did not take the mark*, but successfully resisted.

---

[72] Those who took the mark are further described as experiencing divine judgment forever (Rev 14:9-12)

This is a new thought for a lot of folks, though once we take off our pre-filtered glasses, it's pretty clear in scripture. From this, we can deduce that while the antichrist is powerful, he is not *all*-powerful. His rule is limited in time and scope. He will be resisted, successfully, even by unbelievers.

Five Cities in Egypt

An interesting case-in-point of the limited authority of the antichrist comes from a rather obscure reference to the nation of Egypt in the last days.

> "In that day five cities in Egypt will speak the language of Canaan and swear allegiance to the Lord Almighty...In that day there will be an altar to the Lord in the heart of Egypt, and a monument to the Lord at its border. It will be a sign and witness to the Lord Almighty in the land of Egypt. When they cry out to the Lord because of their oppressors, he will send them a savior and a defender, and he will rescue them. So the Lord will make himself known to the Egyptians, and in that day they will acknowledge the Lord. They will worship with sacrifices and grain offerings; they will make vows to the Lord and keep them." (Isa. 19:18-21, NIV)

Historically, this verse has never been fulfilled, yet one day in the future, five Egyptian cities *will* declare their allegiance to the Lord, even to the point of speaking the language of the Hebrews. Can you imagine such a thing? In simple terms, Egypt is going to experience revival prior to the return of Christ. Follow my logic, because the implications are profound. Due to the future orientation of this verse, along with the particular focus of the Antichrist around the Middle East, we can only assume that this unnamed oppressor is the Antichrist himself. So this extraordinarily powerful dictator, feared by all, operating at the height of his power and geographically positioned near the epicenter of his influence, finds himself utterly unable to control five cities in a poor, developing nation only 300 miles away. Do you see that? We have been trained and conditioned to think that the antichrist is a global despot with totalitarian control, forcing everyone who opposes him to hide in caves like rats, starving from lack of food for three-and-a-half years. But this notion is a myth of man, not a fact of scripture. Does the antichrist wield significant power, perhaps more than any other figure in human history? Possibly, yes.

But that is very different than all-powerful.

What about "The Mark of the Beast"?

So how do we square my assertion with Revelation 13:18, where the beast/antichrist causes "all" to take the mark and worship him? Here we must bear in mind the particular genre of literature into which the book of Revelation falls, for it is not only prophetic in a general sense, but apocalyptic in a specific sense. Classifications of Jewish literature (History, Wisdom, Poetry, Prophetic, Apocalyptic, etc.) have certain distinguishing features, such as clear distinctions in style, content and purpose between modern categories like Crime Noir, Autobiography, Political Memoirs, High Fantasy and Prairie Romance. As such, sometimes events that sound absolute are not what they seem. In Jewish apocalyptic literature, language can be exaggerated, metaphorical, or both, to more dramatically make the point. Absolutes are sometimes symbolic rather than forming a precise mathematical formula.

Let me give you a couple examples. In the first, Daniel 2:39, the prophet is addressing Nebuchadnezzar, ruler of Babylon. This is the very same vision we studied earlier, where Daniel interprets Nebuchadnezzar's dream of a statue with a head of gold, arms of silver, etc.[73] Daniel explains the meaning, which is that several other kingdoms will eventually succeed Babylon, saying, "After you shall arise another kingdom inferior to yours; then another, a third kingdom of bronze, *which shall rule over all the earth*."

The first kingdom was Babylon, the second was Medo-Persia, and the third was the Greek Empire of Alexander the Great. Under the inspiration of the Holy Spirit, Daniel says the Greek Empire would rule over *all* the earth ("whole earth," NIV). Check any number of translations; they share the same all-encompassing language. This becomes problematic only if you insist on imposing a modern, literal understanding upon the text, because, as we know, the Greek Empire did not rule the whole earth. Greece did not rule over North America, Antarctica, South America, Europe, Asia, or most of Africa. It ruled central and eastern Mediterranean, the Middle East, Afghanistan, and even as far as the western edge of India, which is to say, Greece entirely ruled *the world of an Israelite,* so Daniel's prediction was accurate and true. In fact, within its particular frame of reference, Daniel's prophecy was literally true. Yet if we fail to appreciate metaphorical variance, or the particular distinctions of ancient versus modern worldview, or genre, we may go astray by insisting on a rigid, rather than relative, literalism.

Similarly, Daniel 7 describes a "fourth beast" that "will be a fourth kingdom on the earth, which will be different from all the

[73] The book of Daniel is a mixture of History, Prophetic and Apocalyptic genres.

other kingdoms and *will devour the whole earth* and tread it down and crush it." Same thing. If you know the history of the Roman Empire, it did exactly what Daniel described within a total, yet limited scope. The Roman Empire, as large as it was, by no means commanded the totality of seven continents and five oceans. The phrase, "the whole earth," means "the whole of the land," with the primary territory of concern coming from an Israelite perspective. In summary, "whole earth" does not mean "entire planet."[74]

Stars and Saints

I default to a literal interpretation of the Bible because I think it is the safest, wisest way to read scripture. Most of the Bible is literal, including key prophetic passages, yet many portions are clearly metaphorical. In those cases, we have to be careful about forcing exact English interpretations onto nuanced Hebrew phrases and modes of thought, especially when they lack true modern equivalency.

Here's another example. In Matthew 24:29, it says, "Immediately after the tribulations of those days, the sun will be darkened, the moon will not give its light, the stars will fall from heaven, and the powers of heavens will be shaken." Many modern interpreters claim this language indicates either 1) nuclear war or 2) a mass of damaging meteorites falling from the sky. But alternatives exist with similar phrases used elsewhere in the Bible. We must allow scripture to interpret scripture! So when the cruel, antichrist figure

---

[74] Similarly, Daniel 8:5 describes the eventual influence of Alexander the Great as a great, conquering "male goat (coming) from the west, across the surface of the *whole earth.*"

persecuted the saints in Daniel 8, it says he "cast down *some of the host* and *some of the stars to the ground*, and trampled them."

Most scholars believe Antiochus IV Epiphanes, (the Seleucid king who was a Greek descendant of Alexander the Great) was the historical figure who fits Daniel's description and point of reference. His persecutions were a historical series of events. Yet he did not pull stars out of the sky! The Bible is speaking of the saints he killed and murdered. They are like stars being cast down.

It's not a nuclear event. Not a meteor. Not a comet.

Thus, when in Revelation 13 the beast causes "all" to take the mark, we need to employ a discretion too often lacking in the wider Christian prophetic culture. Yes, the dragon gives the antichrist/"beast" power and "great authority." He blasphemes (v. 6) and makes war on the saints (v. 7). But when we read that he has authority "over *every* tribe and people and tongue and nation" (v. 7) and that "*all* who dwell on the earth will worship him" (v. 8), or that "*no one* will be able to buy or to sell" (v. 17), we need to pause and consider the full witness of scripture before jumping to extreme conclusions.

In the midst of my own hybridized view, my primary concern is that hope govern our perspective. The "great tribulation" spoken by Jesus *is* a fact of the past. While Jesus perhaps brilliantly layered His words to include a future fulfillment, it would not change the other facts I've discussed. Namely, the antichrist is clearly portrayed with:

1. Limitations in power and authority. As an example, five entire cities in a nation historically hostile to Israel (Egypt) will not bow to his influence.

2. Limitations in scope. The presence of "sheep and goat nations" at the return of Christ is highly suggestive of a more widespread, global resistance than we've typically imagined. Also, similar, metaphorical language used elsewhere in scripture help us to reframe phrases such as "the whole earth," "every tribe," and "no one able to buy or sell" as possibly a patchwork of regional concentrations, particularly in the area around Israel, rather than total global dominion, unchecked, unmatched.

3. Limitations in duration. Even should you disagree with my reasoning in numbers 1-2 above, scripture clearly limits the *period of time* in which the limited authority and limited scope of the antichrist will rule. He is given three and a half years. (Rev. 13:5-7, also Rev. 11:1-2, comp. to Luke 21:24). That's it. After that, game over.

As you finish this chapter, I can imagine my readers are feeling a mixture of relief and skepticism. There is reason to hope even when a tide of evil crashes on our shores. And perhaps there is also time to see Jesus' earthly harvest come to full fruition.

CHAPTER 8

Reason #8

WE HAVE TIME

Fact:
"You do not know the day nor the hour."
(Matt. 25:13)

A Truly Global Crisis

Current events are wholly untrustworthy predictors of the End. We try to escalate this event or that event to a place of prophetic stature, but most have no such claim. Furthermore, when we stack events so that the sum is greater than the parts, our eschatological quest is often to make headlines global in their net effect. But truly global crises are extremely rare. The most severe period in recent history was probably during the 30 year span from 1914-1945. Historians are free to dispute my opinion, but few periods of time can compare. In fact, if you had lived during this period, you might have thought the world was falling off its hinges, or ending altogether. Below is a summary of everything that went wrong over those three decades.

- 1914, World War I breaks out. Called the "War to End All Wars." Roughly 15 million people from scores of nations perish.
- 1914, chemical warfare erupts across the battlefield for the first time in history.
- 1917, revolution in Russia. A brutal new atheistic political ideology called Communism takes over the largest nation on earth to form a totalitarian regime. They destroy churches and forbid worship. Genocide follows, with estimates as high 60 million people being murdered in the revolution and subsequent political purges.
- 1918, the great influenza (the Spanish Flu). This virulent, highly contagious disease—a true pestilence—kills between 50-100 million people in roughly three years. Nothing like it had been seen since the Black Death.
- 1920s, called "The Flapper Era." This period is known for loose morals, free sexuality, and excessive drinking. Take note: Christians across the nation believed they were under threat as the long-standing traditional morals of the Victorian era suddenly collapsed.
- 1929, Black Monday, the greatest stock market crash in history. Huge amounts of wealth are wiped away. This triggers the Great Depression which gave rise to 20% unemployment across the globe.

- 1939, World War II begins. It lasts for six years and is now known as the deadliest military conflict in history. 60 million people were killed, which represented about 3% of the world population at the time. The infamous Adolf Hitler led the Nazi conquest of Europe, and also implemented "The Final Solution," a terrible ethnic purge of Europe's Jewish population. Approximately eleven million died, most of them Jewish. As such, Hitler is perhaps the clearest picture we have over the last two millennia of a totally demonized, antichrist world ruler.
- 1945, A terrifying new weapon, the nuclear bomb is dropped on Hiroshima, Japan.

Note how many "end of the world" qualities marked this period: great pestilence, economic crisis, war, an immoral falling away, persecution, an Antichrist figure. Yet in spite of so many amazing, prophetic indicators in a compressed period of time, it was not the end. Simply put, *we cannot use world events as signs*, or we will end up like all the other failed predictors trying to force current events into scripture.

Do you remember Hurricane Sandy? Sandy was a 1,100-mile wide storm. That's unbelievably huge! The headlines read, "Biggest Storm in History." Yet depending on where you lived, it probably didn't directly affect you in the slightest. Similarly, those three decades from 1914-1945 either impacted you greatly, or more or less, or not at all. How can there be complete chaos and global mayhem for thirty years, yet people continued getting married, crops were grown, businesses were launched. During one of the worst global convulsions in history, normal life continued.

Now, many probably *thought* the end had come. But then in 1945, the crisis suddenly ended, and what followed was the greatest period of economic and technological growth in all of human history. So many babies were born that they called that generation, "Baby Boomers." The church came roaring to life with a move of God that included the ministry of Billy Graham, the healing revivals of the 1950s, the charismatic renewal in the 1960s, the Jesus Movement in the 1970s, the youth missions movement in the 1980s, and the global prayer movement in the 1990s. Medically and technologically, we have never witnessed such an astonishing period of innovation and advancement.

All of this occurred *after* the world looked like it was over for sure. It's not enough to recognize these facts. We must also let it shift our outlook.

The Tension of Two Imperatives

Regarding His return, Jesus intentionally set up a dynamic tension between two seemingly contradicting imperatives:

1. Stay vigilant, watchful and alert by discerning the times.
2. We can't know the times. "Do business," be productive and fruitful.

As to the former, Jesus criticized the Jews of His day for not recognizing the appearance of their Messiah. "Hypocrites! You can discern the face of the sky and of the earth, but how is it you do not discern this time?" (Luke 12:56). Similarly, they failed to recognize "the time of (their) visitation" (Luke 19:44). Jesus chastised them for their dullness and insensitivity to the many, obvious clues all around. Then in Matthew 24, after rebuking the folks who failed to perceive His first coming, He gave several specific signs to make sure they did not miss His second coming. "Now learn this lesson from the fig tree: As soon as its twigs get tender and its leaves come out, you know that summer is near. Even so, when you see all these things, *you know that it is near, right at the door*" (Matt 24: 32-33, NIV).

Case closed, right? Not at all. As to the second point of tension, Jesus said we *cannot* know the time or season of His return, unequivocally stating this in the very same chapter where He also said we *should* see "these things" and know His coming was right at the door! "Of that day and hour *no one knows*, not even the angels of heaven, nor the Son, but the Father alone" (Matt. 24:36). Later, after His resurrection, Jesus pushed back even more when His disciples "asked Him, saying, 'Lord, will You at this time restore the kingdom to Israel?'…He said to them, 'It is not for you to know times or seasons which the Father has put in His own authority,'" (Acts 1:6-7).

Humans have a need for resolution and meaning, so we tend to infer conclusions and adduce symbolic nuance from events that may be truly random. Our capacity for making omens out of oatmeal is legendary, like silhouettes of Jesus that supposedly appear in a coffee stain or the burn marks of a piece of toast. While wiser disciples may knowingly smirk and dismiss such notions as mere superstition, the burnt toast is little different than the doomsday auguries driving those same, sincere disciples to solve the End-Times like a puzzle. Dispensational "chart tracking" has become an officially sanctioned Christian horoscope. It needs to stop, which is why I believe *Jesus created such deliberate tension between two opposing mindsets*. The point is to be alert and watchful, while simultaneously building for the long-term. So which is it? *Both*. We are *do business*, planning, building, developing, pursuing our God-given dreams, governed by faith not fear—and at the same time, abiding, following, yearning, watching, listening, pursuing a deeper life in God.

The Problem with Imminence

As stated earlier, Dispensationalism imparts a vital, healthy urgency to our faith. However, there are several downsides, including doomsday thinking. Part of this dogma has maintained that, since the first century, the return of Christ has been imminent. Whether they believed in imminence or not is highly subject to debate, but since then, many generations have fully expected the return of Christ.

- Early Church Fathers like Irenaeus and Hippolytus of Rome predicted Jesus would return by 500 AD.
- In 989 AD, during the appearance of Halley's Comet, writers and preachers warned of the soon coming apocalypse, which was expected to arrive at the new millennia. So, come December, 999 AD, worldly goods were sold and given to the poor. Swarms of pilgrims headed east to meet the Lord at Jerusalem. Buildings went unrepaired, crops unplanted, and criminals were set free.
- In 1005-1006 AD, the famine in Europe was viewed apocalyptically. In 1006, a new star appeared. We now know it was a supernova, but when the Church of the Holy Sepulcher in Jerusalem was destroyed by the Muslim Caliph in 1009, it was deemed part of the end of days.

- In 1184, a cadre of astrologers wrote a letter to Pope Clement. This letter circulated throughout Europe, predicting the end of the world in September, 1186. They said there would be wind, storms, drought, famine, pestilences, and earthquakes. Coastal towns would be covered with sand, an event to be triggered by a rare conjunction of planets between the Scales and the tail of the Dragon. People were advised to flee their homes to the mountains. The letter caused panic throughout Europe. The Archbishop of Canterbury ordered a three day fast to prevent the calamity. When September of 1186 arrived, the planetary conjunction did occur, but not the end of the world.
- Pope Innocent III, 1284 AD, predicted the world would end 666 years after the rise of Islam.
- In 1346-51 AD, the Black Plague was interpreted as fulfilling one of the bowls of wrath.
- Christopher Columbus, in his "Book of Prophesies," 1501, predicted the end of the world would occur in 1656.
- Martin Luther predicted the end of the world would occur no later than 1600 AD.
- John Wesley, founder of the Methodist Church, argued that Revelation 12:14 referred to the period of years, 1058-1836 AD. Thus, Wesley anticipated the thousand year reign of Christ to begin in 1836.
- In the mid-1800s, Baptist preacher William Miller was convinced that the second coming of Christ was imminent. After several miscalculations, Miller settled on a firm, final date in October of 1844. Many of his followers, called Millerites left

their jobs and gave away homes and possessions in preparation for the Lord's return, enduring much persecution in the process. This came to be known as "The Great Disappointment."

- William Branham predicted the rapture would happen in 1977.
- Chuck Smith, founder of Calvary Chapel, predicted the generation that started in 1948 would be the last generation. By his calculations, this meant we would see the end by 1981.
- Pat Robertson predicted in 1976 that the world would end in 1982.
- Lester Sumrall predicted the same for 1985.
- Harold Camping made international headlines for his repeatedly failed predictions that Jesus would return, first on May 21, 2011, later revised to Oct. 21, 2011.
- Not to be outdone, in 2014-2015, Mark Blitz and John Hagee began predicting that the end would begin in 2015.

One thing is sure. We like to predict!

Many of these are eminent and godly people, and some even excellent theologians. But they all succumbed to the temptation to prophetically interpret the current events of their day. Not only do they have to live with the humiliation of looking foolish, but also the irreparable harm they have caused to the millions of faithful followers who stopped *doing business* because of their predictions.

The Problem with Urgency

Imminence produces urgency. Admittedly, this can yield a certain emotional vibrancy to our walk with God, but the negatives outweigh the positives. The Doctrine of Imminence greatly contributes to short-term mindsets. Christians are practicing so much urgency that we refuse to plan anything requiring long-term vision or commitment.

Yet the Bible is clear: "The plans of the diligent lead to profit as surely as haste leads to poverty" (Prov. 21:5, NIV). True to form, the Christian community proves the point. Not only is our impact in society rather impoverished, but our individual lives are often impoverished, as well.

In this book, I have not been shy to admit that there will always be challenges and difficulties. That's precisely the point. Essentially, Solomon was telling us, "Get used to it. Settle into the kind of life where you make plans for the long haul. Life has trouble. Nations will experience trouble. Patience, perseverance and long-term thinking is the only way to prosper."

In other words, don't be too "hasty" (i.e. short-term) with your thinking. Don't be tempted to accelerate time. If you think that way, you'll make mistakes, you'll miss opportunities, and you'll have the wrong perspective.

In the next section, I'm going to give you two key reasons I am convinced our hasty eschatology is wrong.

Two Key Indicators that Now is not the Time

First. Babylon. Revelation chapters 17-18 describe Babylon in three key ways:

1. *A false religion ("Mother of Harlots").* In the Bible, harlotry always refers to mixture, unfaithfulness, and false religion. This description conveys an amalgamation of religion. Some call this future Babylon a "one-world religion."

2. *A city.* It's also a literal city, and a great city—one of the greatest on the whole earth. Babylon is described as a *city that reigns over kings*. In scope, it sounds like a rival to London, New York, or Tokyo. It's a gigantic, influential city.

3. *An economic system.* Babylon becomes one of the greatest economic centers in the earth, controlled by the greatest merchants in the earth. In fact, Babylon will be so great that when it finally falls, all the great shipmasters and merchants of the earth will witness the event with weeping and awe. The implication is Babylon's fall means economic ruin.

A religious system, a city, and an economic system, all in one. That's confusing to the modern mind. The best portrait I can offer is that of the medieval Catholic Church. Please note, I am not attempting to equate the modern Catholic Church with the whore of Babylon, an equivalence many have attempted in the past. Yet during the Medieval Ages, at least, it certainly fit the bill: it was an economic system and a religion; and Rome was simultaneously one of the world's most dominant cities. It was perhaps the closest type or symbol of Babylon in history.

But the Book of Revelation says another Babylon coming, wielding influence that will spread across the earth before it is eventually destroyed by the Antichrist. Here's the problem for hasty eschatology. Where's this Babylon today? Where is it? *I don't see it.* If the end is imminent, then we should be able to clearly identify a Babylon that fits those three criteria. Where is this literal city with broad and heretical religious control, and massive economic power?

If you take the Bible literally, then you have a while until Jesus returns, because Babylon will have to be rebuilt into a huge city, worldwide religion, and an economic system.

Figure 12 Ancient Babylon Today

Today, ancient Babylon is basically a pile of ruins in the middle of a desert. [75] In terms of engineering and infrastructure, cities

---

[75] A popular alternate case has been made by many that Babylon is the city of Rome (ref. 1 Pet. 5:13), or the more broadly stated "Revived Roman Empire," meaning Europe. In this case, a deeply secularized, atheistic Europe would have to

like Jakarta and Hong Kong have massively expanded over the last three to four decades, but that is purely a function of construction and manpower.

Perhaps the most remarkable city to literally rise out of the desert is Dubai. In a matter of twenty years, this United Arab Emirates city has become a world destination. Yet in those twenty years, while an entire city miraculously rose from the sands, Dubai is in no way a global market or a religious empire. So at minimum, we are looking at a period of decades to both accrue and wield that kind of influence. It takes a long time for nations to become economic powers, much less individual cities. It takes a long time for religions to rise to the stature of international loyalties. More realistically, the raw power ascribed to Babylon will take centuries.

In short, it's a ways off. Don't get caught in short-term thinking.

Second. The Jewish Temple. The other major impediment to imminence is that according to most Dispensational teaching,[76] in order for the abomination of desolation to occur—wherein a literal idol will be placed inside the Holy of Holies—an actual temple is required. In Jerusalem.

But there is no temple in Jerusalem, which means the Jewish temple would have to be *rebuilt.*

As you can imagine, this is no small task. In order for the Jewish temple to be rebuilt, an agreement would have to be bro-

---

become profoundly religious again. In either event—Rome as Babylon, or Babylon as Babylon—it would seem we are a long way off.

[76] As stated in the previous chapter, I am not convinced another temple is required to be rebuilt.

kered between Jews and the Muslims who now control the Temple Mount in Jerusalem. This deal would effectively permit Israel to replace the Al-Aqsa Mosque with a historic, Jewish religious structure. The very thought would inflame every Muslim nation which would consider it to be a personal affront to Mohammed, who supposedly ascended to heaven from that location. For this reason, Jerusalem is the third holiest city in Islam, ranked only behind Mecca and Medina. Do you know how many peace agreements have been attempted in that region, how much blood has been spilled, how deeply humiliated and begrudging the surrounding Arab nations still feel after their losses in 1948 and 1967? Do you know how much racial hatred and ancient animosity exists between those peoples? I'm not saying it couldn't happen.

I'm saying it will *take time.*

(A third characteristic, which I define as the current and projected state of the church, also forces us to extend our otherwise hasty expectations, but I will deal with that topic in the final chapter).

The Greatest Sign of All

The greatest and most authentic sign we should seek is the manifestation of the fully matured Kingdom of God.

> "And He said, 'The Kingdom of God is as a man should scatter seed in the ground, and sleep by night or day and rise by day, but the seed should sprout and grow; he himself does not know how. For the earth yields its crops by itself, first the blade, then the head, then the full grain in the head. <u>When</u>

> the grain ripens, he immediately puts it in the sickle because then the harvest has come'" (Mark 4:26-29)

There's a progression from seed to blade to grain to the early head of grain to full grain in the head...*then* the harvest. Where are we in this progression? How long will it take to get to full, historic harvest? This is a barometer for timing, because Jesus is not coming back until the full grain is grown, meaning the total fruit of everything He meant to achieve through the planting of the seed of His own life.

What farmer plants a crop, then as soon as the first sprouts appear attempts to harvest? *The entire point of planting a crop is the harvest.* God is no fool, and He is simply not harvesting the earth until His crop is 100% ripe. Otherwise the seed is sown in vain, which the Father would never allow.

He's not bluffing. He wants a mature kingdom and full harvest. Look at the list at the start of the next chapter. *Nothing* of His perfect purpose will be found lacking. And only *then* shall come the harvest, but certainly not before. Thus, do you see? The process of completion, fruition and manifestation has yet to happen, and would seem to be a good ways off if we are honest. Therefore, if God is patient and willing to wait until the full manifestation, full fruitfulness and full harvest, we must be willing to wait, as well.

> "[7]Therefore be patient, brethren, until the coming of the Lord. The farmer waits for the precious produce of the soil, being patient about it, until it gets the early and late rains. [8]You too be patient; strengthen your hearts, for the coming of the Lord is near" (James 5:7-8).

It's a paradox. It's *near*. It was near then, when James first said it. That's been two thousand years! So be patient. Don't be hasty.

> "But do not let this one fact escape your notice, beloved, that with the Lord one day is like a thousand years, and a thousand years like one day. The Lord is not slow about His promise, as some count slowness, but is patient toward you, not wishing for any to perish but for all to come to repentance" (2 Pet. 3:8-9).

Yes, it has been far longer than most people would ever have expected. It is probably going to be longer still, and in my view, potentially centuries. Obviously, some things are in place that have never been before, but some prophetic keystones remain absent. Take a deep breath and start thinking long-term. We've got some time.

There Is Continuity between This Age and the Next

There are probably many generations until the final generation. But even if Jesus does return immediately, there is still no cause for short-term thinking, because there is actually continuity between this age and the next!

The traditional Christian mindset is of preparing for a disembodied heavenly existence, which makes all earthly pursuits temporary and pointless. Nothing could be further from the truth! As you shall see, when He does come, there's a continuity between this age and the next that should both inspire and release you to invest *now* for the sake of an even more profitable return *then*.

Bluntly stated, you *should* build your business, grow your family, launch your ministry, invest in your career, get that college degree, buy property or stock, get involved in a startup, build a business, do missions work, visit another culture. Get busy with life. Why? Because for the believer, *life never ends.*

When Jesus initiated the Great Commission, He said go into all the nations, preach the Gospel and make disciples of all nations. Implicit in the understanding of His return is the notion that it's not all wiped away, it's not all zeroed out. *Rather than destroy our labors, the Lord intends to honor, uphold, reward and build upon them.* When Peter, Paul and other first century visionaries began a work, they understood that when Jesus returned, their work would not be erased—it would be the very foundation of what was to come! In fact, when you *do business*, you build upon their labor, just as your children will build upon yours. The saints of God uniquely enjoy the privilege of continuity between the generations and the ages; that's why the "cloud of witnesses" (Heb. 12:1) bears eager witness to our efforts, because "apart from us they (cannot) be made perfect" (Heb. 11:40).

The coming shaking (Heb. 12:26-27) targets only the shakable, with the point being to *preserve unharmed that which cannot be shaken.* This speaks to the enduring permanence of eternal service. Nations will shake. Governments will shift. Powerful men will rise and fall. But the Word of the Lord and the eternal kingdom will endure forever. When we participate in putting that kingdom into an earthly context, we are sowing seed that will eventually mature into something unshakeable.

It will endure, continue (i.e. continuity) from this age straight into the next. Jesus will return, but your job and mission will continue. Do you see the perils of hasty, short-term thinking? I want to be well-positioned at His return to begin the next phase of productivity. I don't want to start from scratch. I want tools in my tool belt!

This continuity has implications for our labors in prayer, in business, in leadership, in character development and relational wholeness, as well as art, science, policy and law. The prayers we make, is intercession which will last. Our social impact, legislation, justice initiatives and dynamic social institutions will all be remembered. What William Wilberforce did will remain—we build on it today, and it will continue to be built upon in the next age. *Anything* we reform will be the foundation built upon. Inventions, innovations, and scientific breakthroughs can never be unlearned. Understanding gained, knowledge learned, skills developed, will all transcend. Natural accomplishments, physical architecture, highways, bridges and other technologies will continue. Some say they will not. I say, are you so sure? The more we reshape these things into reflections of the divine ways of God, the more our fruitfulness remains.

"You did not choose Me but I chose you, and appointed you that you would go and bear fruit, *and that your fruit would remain*" (John 15:16).

God actually desires that our impact remain. He wants to sustain, not destroy it. He desires that His own image—in us!—would grow and produce impact on the same order of timelessness and eternality as Himself.

When you fully absorb the impact of these truths, when these eight reasons for our great future get burned into your soul, one beautiful, unavoidable impulse remains: hope.[77]

If you wish to stick to your guns on imminent Dispensationalism as a theological framework, please do! Just add hope. Steep it in hope. Saturate it in hope and expectation of good. Focus on God, not the Antichrist. Stare into the Kingdom of God, not Satan. Think about how to bring the light, not how bad the darkness is. Be the Joshua and Caleb warriors, not the 10-spies wimps.

We have a lot to do, and we will never make the attempt if we are certain the results are doomed to fail. Jesus wants a *full* return on His mighty salvation investment, thus the *full* delay. If it is possible (and it is according to 2 Pet. 3:12), let's speed up the process with the most massive kingdom hope invasion ever.

Jesus called this life—your life—"a little thing." The real action is in the next age! But *this* age is where you put on your skills and learn and grow in preparation for it. The end of the story is His to tell, but the faithful will inherit all things with Him. Our job is to be productive and fruitful, to do our part in the light business. This is why the greatest enemy to our destiny is short-term thinking. Let's root it out.

For those who do, untold wonders await. This is the true hope of His return.

---

[77] Some critics may object by falsely claiming that I am a doubter on the order of 2 Peter 3:4, joining the scoffers who say, "What happened to the promise of His coming?" Far from it! Rather, in either event, should His return come tomorrow or in a hundred years, is uniquely the Father's decision and the Son's job. Meanwhile, *my* job, and yours, between those two unknowns, is to get busy on the planet (ref. Matt 25, Luke 19).

CHAPTER 9

THE HOPE OF HIS RETURN

"Looking for the blessed hope and glorious appearing of our great God and Savior Jesus Christ." (Titus 2:13)

The Glorious Church

In closing, having addressed and hopefully established eight reasons for hope in our future, it is time to turn our attention to one powerful fact: Jesus promised a glorious, empowered, unified church before His return. We've spent a lot of time on evil, danger and antichrist, but scripture gives much more attention to the power and fulfillment of Christ's own body than to the terrible reign of any future beast. Before Christ returns, we are promised to come into:

1. Unbroken communion in horizontal and vertical unity (John 17)
2. To the measure of the stature of the fullness of Christ (Philippians 3)
3. Unto a corporate, mature man, fully equipped (Ephesians 4)
4. With families operating in relational wholeness (Luke 1:17)
5. With authority over creation as sons of God (Romans 8)
6. Demonstrating greater works than Jesus (John 14:12)
7. Prepared as a pure, spotless Bride, ready for our Bridegroom (Revelation 22:2)
8. So that the gates of death no longer prevail (Matthew 16)
9. And the gospel *of the Kingdom* is preached in all the world (Matthew 24:14)
10. And the Great Commission is fulfilled (Matthew 28)
11. And the Kingdom of God is fully ripened (Mark 4:26-29)
12. Until the whole lump is leavened (Luke 13:20)
13. Until the "stone cut without hands" "becomes a great mountain and fills the whole earth" (Daniel 2:34-35)

The implication is that the most powerful, united network of power and light will come from *us*, the church! God's people will rise together with an anointing of unprecedented grace, ingenuity and authority. What would it be like to *look and act like Jesus*, to possess His unbelievable wisdom in every situation, to move in signs and wonders with authority over creation? What if this dramatic anointing of wisdom, love and power is no longer concentrated in one person, as in the days of Jesus, but expressed as a corporate anointing involving millions of believers?

Good news! Scripture promises that very thing. The power and influence of the church has been *greatly underestimated.*

Returning To Hope

As I shared way back in Chapter One, first century disciples were not dreading the second coming, but were very excited about it! Paul wrote about "the *blessed hope and glorious appearing* of our great God and Savior Jesus Christ" (Titus 2:13). The writer of Hebrews wrote of *eagerness* in awaiting *full salvation*:

> "Christ will appear a second time, not to carry any burden of sin...but to bring to <u>full salvation</u> those who are <u>[eagerly, constantly, and patiently]</u> waiting for and expecting Him" (Heb. 9:28, AMP).

Hear the excitement, eagerness, anticipation! Let me ask you: do you feel eager and excited when you consider His return, or is it buried under layers of dread? First century believers were deeply excited. It wasn't a heavy, fearful thing, it was an event to which they looked forward. The early disciples rejoiced because they anticipated the extraordinary hidden bounty that would accompany Christ's return: *full salvation.*

Modern Christian vernacular equates being born again to being saved. But in the fullness of the Biblical concept, our salvation is not yet complete. Peter said we are being "kept by the power of God, through faith for salvation ready to be revealed at the last time" (1 Pet. 1:3-5). To the Roman believers, he said, "Our salvation is nearer now than when we first believed" (Rom. 13:11).

Salvation is getting nearer? If you're saved, it's already here, right? And yet it is getting nearer. Perhaps, like I once did, you totally miss the point of these verses. What is Paul saying? When I began to dig deeper, my discoveries left me undone. Let me tell you, the study of ultimate salvation rapidly became one of the most exciting studies I've ever done in my life. Wow...*salvation*!

Below, in closing, I'm going to summarize sixteen dynamic dimensions of salvation. Some are pretty basic. We take them for granted. But as you advance through the list, you're going to be confronted with progressively shocking, outrageous, wonderful dimensions of salvation that you might have never fully considered. May these sixteen factors of fullness in the church and the ultimate hope of our salvation be the death knell of fearful dogma in your life!

Sixteen Wonders of Ultimate Salvation

1. Resurrection from the dead. Paul said "there will be a resurrection of both the righteous and the wicked" (Acts 24:15). If you've died, you're going to be resurrected.

2. Eternal life. "Whoever should believe in Him should not perish, but have eternal life" (John 3:16). We're not just going to be resurrected from the dead; we're going to live forever.

3. Adoption as sons. We're actually going to be adopted into the divine family. "We ourselves, having the first fruits of the Spirit wait eagerly for our adoption as sons" (Rom. 8:23). In the full view of this verse, we're saved as a matter of position, grace and

choice, but our full placement into the family of God has not yet occurred. If you will, the adoptions papers have been signed, the law is on our side, but we haven't been taken home. Our full royal privilege as sons of God is yet to be realized.

4. Redemption of our bodies. Forgive me, but this is extremely cool. "We eagerly await...the Lord Jesus Christ, who...will transform our lowly bodies so that they *will be like his glorious body*" (Phil 3:20-21). Jesus died, and when He was raised, He got a new, deathless, perfect body. We will, too, just like His! We will not be disembodied spirits as most believe! Jesus' new body was physical: they recognized Him, they touched Him, and He ate fish—but he also walked through walls![78]

And your new body, and mine, will be incorruptible, glorious, powerful and spiritual. Never again will we get sick, or waste away, or die.

> [41]...The body is sown in corruption, it is raised in incorruption. [43]It is sown in dishonor, it is raised in glory. It is sown in weakness, it is raised in power. [44]It is sown a natural body, it is raised a spiritual body. (1 Cor. 15:41-44, NKJV)

5. Redemption of creation. We're going to see the natural order of creation itself liberated from bondage and decay (Rom. 8:21). No, creation is not some conscious, self-aware entity, yet within the limited capacity of human language to express it, creation is *frustrated* because of sin. Jesus has pledged to fix this. I remember vacationing near a beautiful forest, approaching some of the lush vegetation and thinking how beautiful and perfect it was.

---

[78] John 20:19-31, Luke 24:36-53. See also Rom. 8:23, 1 Cor. 15:51-53

But then I got closer noticed how rotten many of the individual leaves were. The contaminated state of creation is on borrowed time. Soon, all will be renewed, reborn, redeemed. You and I have *never lived in a pristine, unfallen world*, but we shall!

6. Unlimited revelation of Jesus. "For now we see in a mirror dimly, but then face to face," which means "we shall see Him as He is," for when "Jesus will be revealed from Heaven" it is "to be glorified in His saints" (1 Cor. 13:12; 1 John 3:2; 2 Thes. 7, 10).

His coming will grant us a complete revelation of who He is. Our faith will become sight. The full, unguarded display of His attributes will stun the globe, and capture our affection at the deepest levels imaginable. We will be completely rapt in awe and undone. It says He shall be called, "Wonderful" (Is .9:6); Jesus will be seen as the "Desired of the nations" (Hag 2:7); and the "sun will be ashamed and the moon disgraced" by His beauty (Is 24:23).

7. Total transformation. "When Christ appears, we shall be like him, for we shall see him as He is" (1 John 3:2, NIV). We will be completely transformed into His image. No more flesh, no more stumbling.

8. Union with Him. "If I go and prepare a place for you, I will come again and receive you to Myself, that where I am, there you may be also" (John 14:3). We're going to reside with Him. No more separation. No more distance. We will "live together with Him and share His life" (1 Thes. 5:10) and "we shall always be with the Lord" (1 Thes. 4:17). We, who have been given to him, will be "with Him, where He is" (John 17:24). Closeness and unbroken, unashamed intimacy with Christ—that's our future. Remember, all these points are talking about *ultimate salvation.*

Heaven is not bliss because of its location. It's bliss because it's where He dwells! Finally, the human potential to live together with God, share His life, be one with Him in the same family and household, will be realized. How do the mechanics work that we rule on earth yet never depart from Jesus? I don't have a clue, but I can't wait to find out!

9. Full of grace. "Fix your hope completely on the grace to be brought to you at the revelation of Jesus Christ" (1 Pet. 1:13). No more second-guessing His love, no more condemnation or shame. The full, unlimited confidence of grace will be ours, because He will bring it to us.

10. Joy. "But rejoice inasmuch as you participate in the sufferings of Christ, so that you may be *overjoyed* when his glory is revealed" (1 Pet. 4:13). There will be crazy, exploding joy in our souls at His triumphant return, and joy in His unrestricted presence (Ps 16:11). Joy like you have never experienced before, joy that could not be any greater! That's what *fullness* means.

11. Incorruptible inheritance. "Blessed be the God and Father of our Lord Jesus Christ, who…has caused us to…obtain an inheritance which is imperishable and undefiled and will not fade away, reserved in heaven for you" (1 Pet. 1:3-4). Not only are you going to receive a shocking, glorious inheritance, but it can never be taken away. Ever. We take these things for granted, but they are meant to fix our soul with hope on His return. These things sustain us through challenges and tears.

12. Reward. "Behold, I am coming soon, and I shall bring My wages and rewards with Me, to repay and render to each one just what his own actions and his own work merit" (Rev. 22:12, AMP;

also Matt. 16:27). There are some rewards like forgiveness and eternal life that are granted to all identically. But there are others that are granted uniquely to each individual, based on our earthly life (Matt. 25:14-30, Luke 19:11-27).

In 2 Corinthians 5:10, standing before the judgment seat to receive rewards, the concept is compared to an athlete, having finished his race, who stands before the Olympic judges waiting for his medal. Paul viewed life as a long race that resulted in a final appearance before the judge. He's going to look at what you did, but even more, He's going to judge what was in your heart. I love this because only God could know what's in a person's heart. *Why* did you do that thing? It looked glorious to others, and you received a lot of praise, but why did you do it? Likewise, that thing you did only for Him, when nobody was watching, He saw it. He knows. On that day, even if you forgot that little act of mercy or generosity, He'll remember. It is all part of salvation, and it will last forever.

I'm spending more time on this particular facet of salvation because we need to understand that rewards are part of the eternal design of God. We should not be afraid. This does not base salvation on works, but it enhances the value of our boldness in faith. We should seek rewards. A good payday is part of the hope of His coming!

> "Rejoice and be exceedingly glad for great is your reward in Heaven" (Matt. 5:12).

13. Glorification and honor. As an extension of the concept of reward, there are also different levels and types of glory. "There are also heavenly bodies and earthly bodies, but the glory of the

heavenly is one, and the glory of the earthly is another. There is one glory of the sun, and another glory of the moon, and another glory of the stars; for star differs from star in glory. *So also is the resurrection of the dead*" (1 Cor. 15: 40-42).

Did you get that? The moon is bright, but the sun is far brighter. The stars vary in brightness. Different levels of glory await us. It's all good, it's all glorious. But it will be infinitely unique. Who are these glorious ones? They are the future redeemed, fully adopted, resurrected, glorified sons of God. If you are saved, then when you are fully saved, the Bible says Creation can't wait to meet you!

"The earnest expectation of creation eagerly waits for the revealing of the sons of God" (Rom. 8:19). The glory you will carry, embody and reveal, will be stunning beyond human language, beyond poetry, beyond conceivability. Jesus said it this way, "The righteous will shine forth as the sun in the kingdom of their Father" (Matt. 13:43). Daniel said it this way, "Those who are wise will shine like the brightness of the firmament and those who turn many to righteousness like the stars forever" (Dan. 12:3). Wow, your choices now make that kind of difference…forever!

Right now, you know yourself pretty well—good, bad and ugly. Warts and all, you're you. But in another sense, you have no idea who you are, because you have no idea how Christ really perceives you through His eyes of love. But when He comes, He will reveal the amazing, beautiful you that He sees. "When Christ, who is our life, is revealed, then you also will be revealed with Him in glory" (Col. 3:4). So when He is revealed, He will also reveal the glory of each of us, for the very first time.

14. A new name. Personally, this one intrigues me. "The one who is victorious I will make a pillar in the temple of my God. Never again will they leave it. I will write on them the name of my God and the name of the city of my God, the new Jerusalem, which is coming down out of heaven from my God; and *I will also write on them my new name*" (Rev. 3:12, NIV).

I believe this new name will occur when God personally testifies of our life and faith, our trust in Him. This is when Papa brags on His kids before all the angels. He says something like this, "Let me tell you about Susan. Let me tell you how she lived her life. Let me tell you the choices she made. Let me tell you when the hard things happened, how she lived and how she chose me." He's going to tell the secret stories that no one else knew.

And then when it is all done, like a title for victor, a secret whispered between best friends, or a loving pet name given to a child, our new name will unfold and confirm the wonders of His reality within us. This is when we are truly joined. Our names become part of His name. Susan the Forgiver or Susan the Gracious, or some Hebrew name that's a thousand, thousand words long, but we instantly remember it. Or a secret tongue of angels that only God knows, but He lets us in on the sound of our own name. I don't know, I'm speculating, but the fact that He will go to this step, this otherwise unnecessary, almost throw away step, reveals exactly the opposite—how nothing gets lost, how carefully He will pay attention to every detail on that day, and how carefully He knows and loves us. It will be like a kiss that brands our soul forever with fire and identity for all eternity.

All of these wonders are urging us on to believe, risk, and dare greatly. These are tokens of hope, to root us on. Be done with fearful dread, depression and despair! Heaven is rooting you on. Angels are cheering. You can do it! You can forgive, you can rise up, you can endure! You can love, you can enjoy, you can be at peace! You can conquer addiction, you can give beyond measure, you can hope beyond fear! Jesus Himself is rooting for us because He wants these things to manifest in our life now, preparing us for the day when faith becomes sight. He has a secret name for you. Do you want to know it? I do! It is the final token of your acceptance by God and title to glory.

15. Crowns. Among others, the Bible talks about crowns of righteousness, life and glory. For suffering unto death as the innocent Lamb of God, Jesus Himself was crowned with glory and honor. "Do you not know that in a race all the runners run, but only one gets the prize? Run in such a way as to get the prize. They do it to get a crown that will not last, but we do it to get a crown that will last forever" (1 Cor. 9:24-25).

> "Blessed is the man who endures temptation, for when he has been approved, he will receive the crown of life, which the Lord has promised to those who love Him" (James 1:17).

Peter told his flock that "when the shepherd appears, you will receive the crown of glory that does not fade away" (1 Pet. 5:4).

The Bible also talks about jewels and gold and precious stones. It's about special garments. I think they are literal! Why? Because we will have *physical* bodies to put them on! But whether these things are literal or symbolic, they are real and rich and rewarding. I want them. Why tell us about them if it is sinful to desire them? If He plans on giving them anyway, He could have spared us the details until the day of delivery. I believe this indicates that He want us to be motivated by these things.

16. Rulership. "You have made them to be a kingdom and priests to our God; and they will reign upon the earth" (Rev. 5:10). As heirs, the faithful will rule and reign with Him forever. The aforementioned crowns actually picture this reality, for naturally, people with crowns are rulers of something! In fact, rulership is far more glorious than a crown. By assigning us to significant roles, God's appointment of influence and authority is one of the greatest gifts He could possibly give. It's unique to every individual and based entirely on the way we've lived our life (see Luke 19:11-27; 2 Timothy 2:12; Rev. 2:26, 21:7).

This is our opportunity. If we're His children, we are also His heirs (Rom. 8:17). Jesus is heir to the entire earth and universe. How big is the playground of your future? As big as the title deed held by the only begotten Son of God. He will joyfully share His inheritance with us.

Perhaps now you get why the Bible calls the day of His return "our blessed hope?" It is precisely because of these sixteen things. They fulfill the promise of history. They will usher us into a new age. Yes, it will be glorious and good then, but it's also good *now*.

Hope Here, Hope Now

If you haven't tasted it yet, I'm not sure how to sweeten the recipe. I've tried to provide the right mix of cold, hard statistics from a scientific and historic point of view. But I've also grounded every concept in the infallible Word of God. Have you tasted the sweetness and beauty of that word, hope?

I don't want to keep banging away at the Christian doomsday culture. Actually, I want to leave it behind. I believe God is inviting us to have hope in His return that translates to real, nitty-gritty, stubbornly optimistic happiness and hope in this age. Hope is our confident expectation that more and more good lies ahead, and that no amount of bad can change that. With hope, we wait for full salvation with joy and zing. We dance more. We give more. We sing and build more. To the modern, jaded way of thinking, hope has become synonymous with an unlikely possibility only a fool would believe, i.e. "Yeah, right, fat chance." I *hope* I win the lottery, which is practically guaranteed to mean I won't.

No, no, no! Biblical hope is the full, confident expectation of good. We live in the day of His favor. There's a lot of bad stuff out there, but hope tells us, in modern parlance, *it's all good.* He wins. And we win. Because His reward is with Him

The pessimism and dread I've addressed in this book are deeply entrenched. We need to expunge our destructive doctrine of despair and move into a new dawn of transformational power. If this book has been successful, then maybe, just maybe, there is one less adherent to hopelessness, and one more person ready to engage the world for good.

My friend Bob Hartley had a dream a few years back. In his night vision, Bob asked the Lord to show him his city in the year 2020. At the time, 2020 was many years in the future. Bob was shown a horrible, apocalyptic city, and it was his hometown. Darkness was everywhere, along with fear and terror. This confirmed his expectations—it was exactly what he thought would happen! Then all of a sudden, the vision flipped and he saw a glorious city full of light, joy, love, justice and godly activity. It was beautiful in every sense of the word.

In the dream, Bob was confused and asked a question, "Lord, which is it? Which is real?"

The Lord answered, "*You decide*."

Bob said emphatically, "I choose the good one!!!"

The Lord said, "Good. It's done."

We are the light of the world. But if we believe the city is doomed, we stand by and let it go to its doom. We hide our light in our bunkers. It becomes a self-fulfilling prophecy. But if we hope in the future, turn up our light, and put it on display, light comes. Darkness recedes. The world is transformed, inch by inch.

I return again to the Two Spies, Joshua and Caleb, who simply believed God was greater than the giants and the fortified cities in front of them.

Let's join them.

It's a rich life. You are living your gift. Seize your opportunity. Renounce fear. Choose faith. Never stop hoping for the better thing to come (Eph. 1:8; 1 Thes. 5:8; Rom. 5:5).

Until that final day, we've got work to do. Every light counts, as we now find ourselves at that point where heaven and earth meet—the *Kingdom Horizon*.

APPENDIX

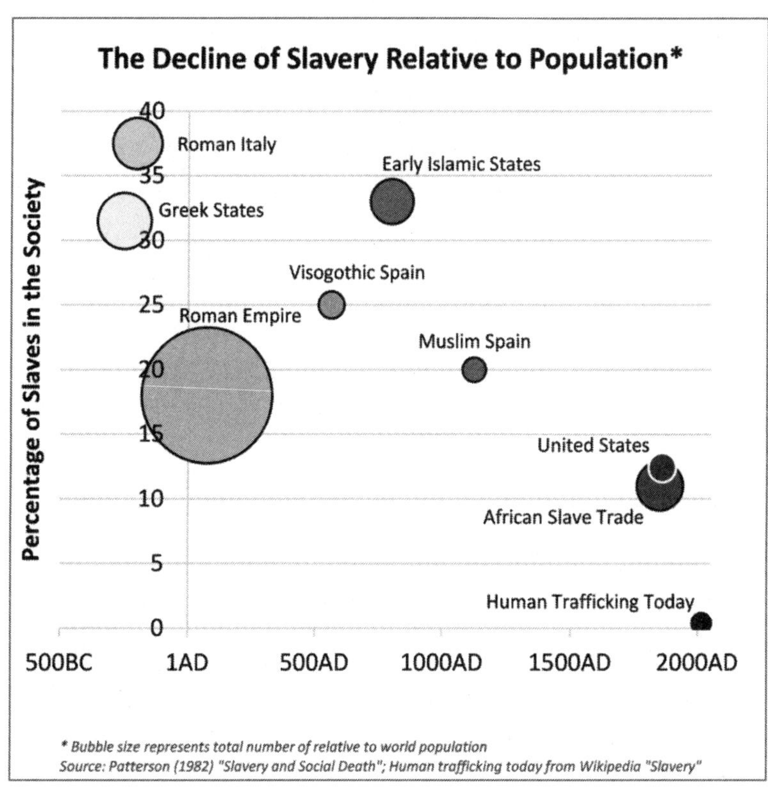

Figure 13 Decline of Slavery

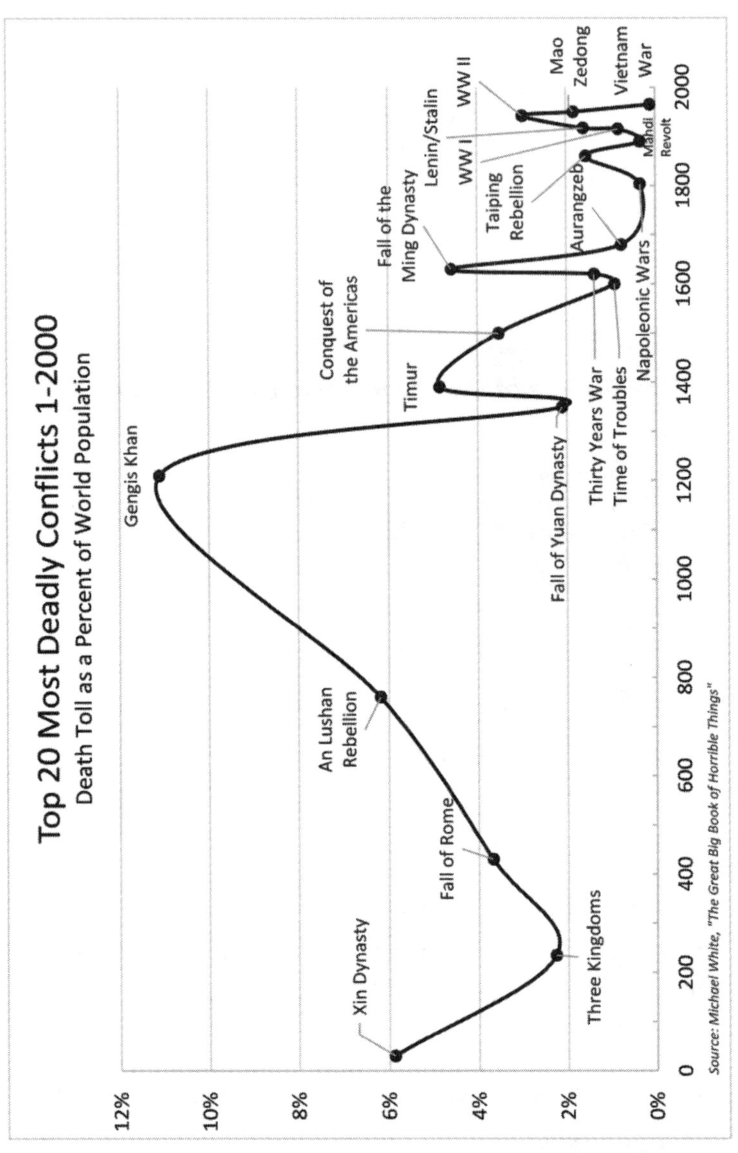

Figure 14 Global Deaths in Conflict

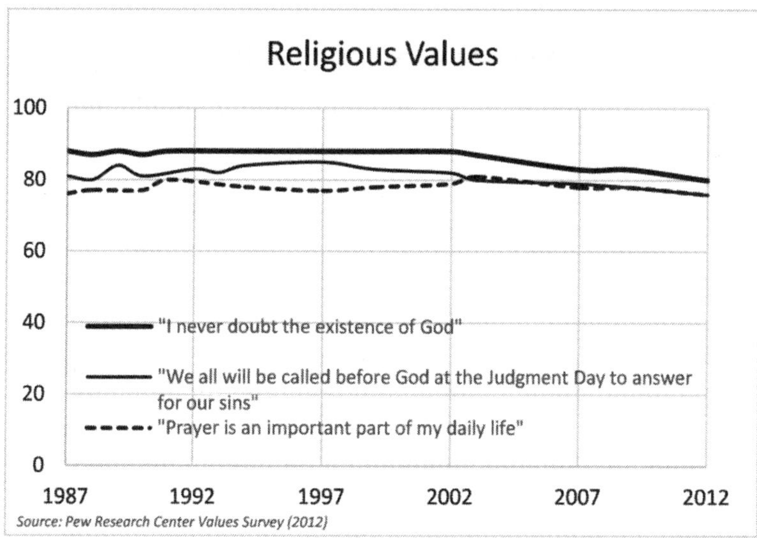

Figure 15 Religious Values in the US

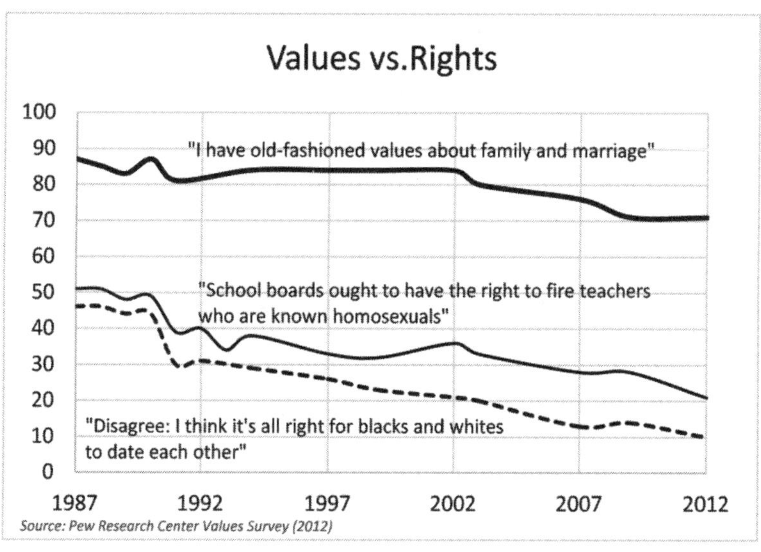

Figure 16 Values vs. Rights in the US

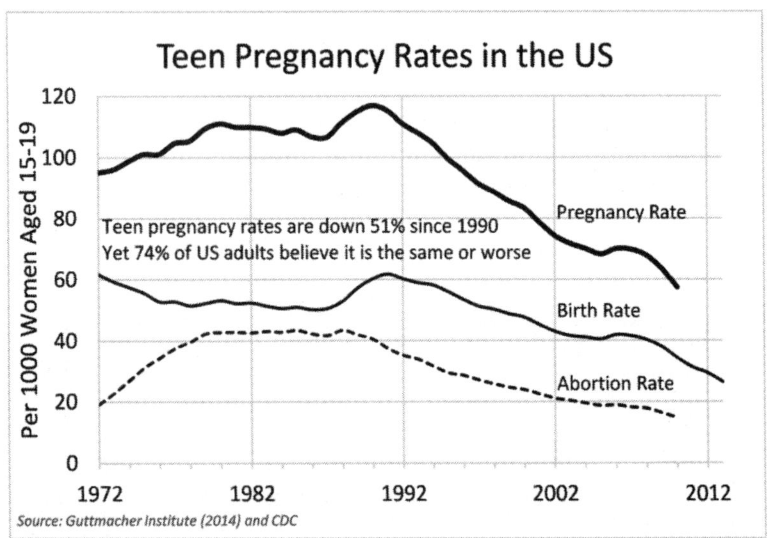

Figure 17 Teen Pregnancy Rates in the US

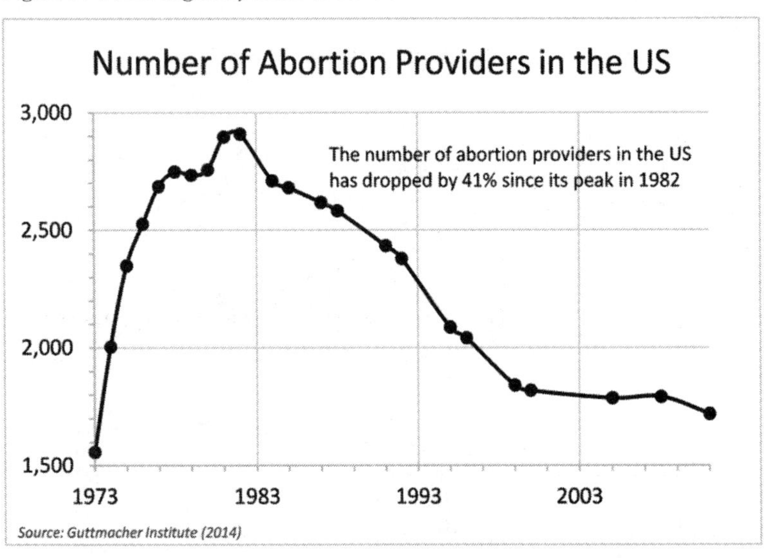

Figure 18 Number of Abortion Providers in the US

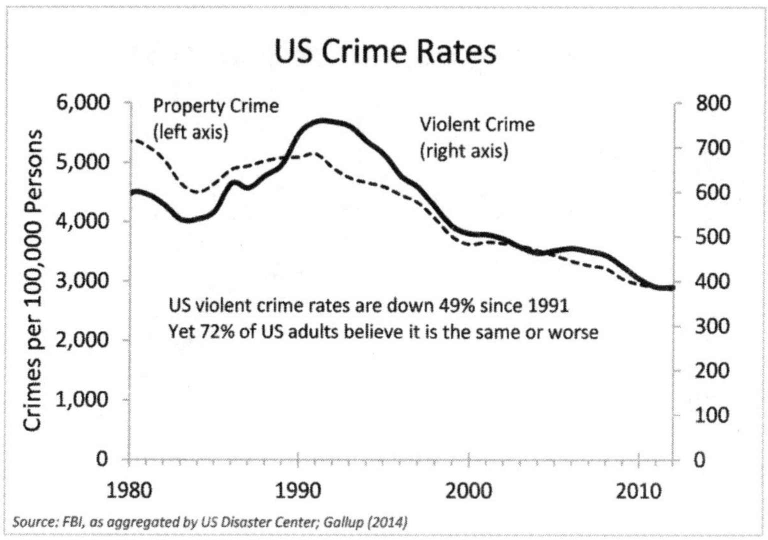

Figure 19 US Crime Rates

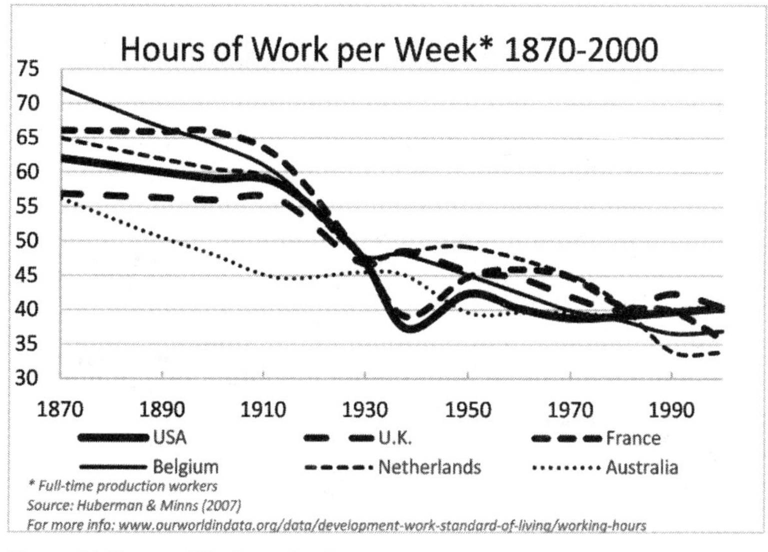

Figure 20 Hours of Work per Week

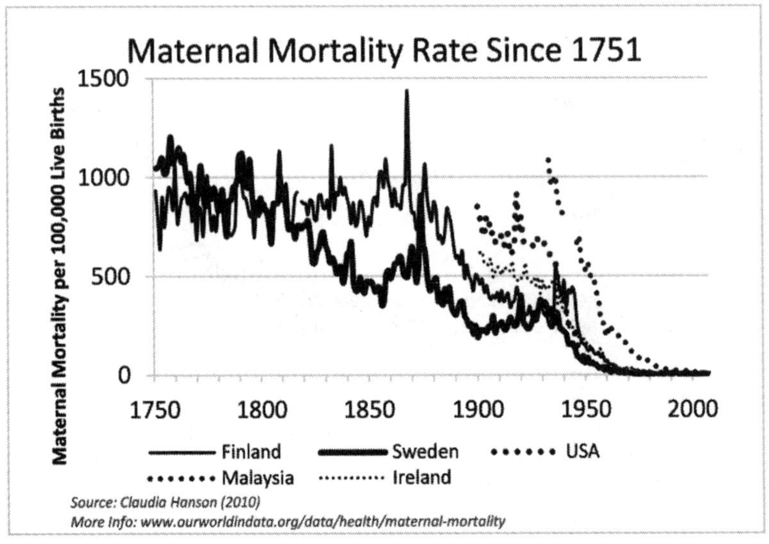

Figure 21 Maternal Mortality Rates

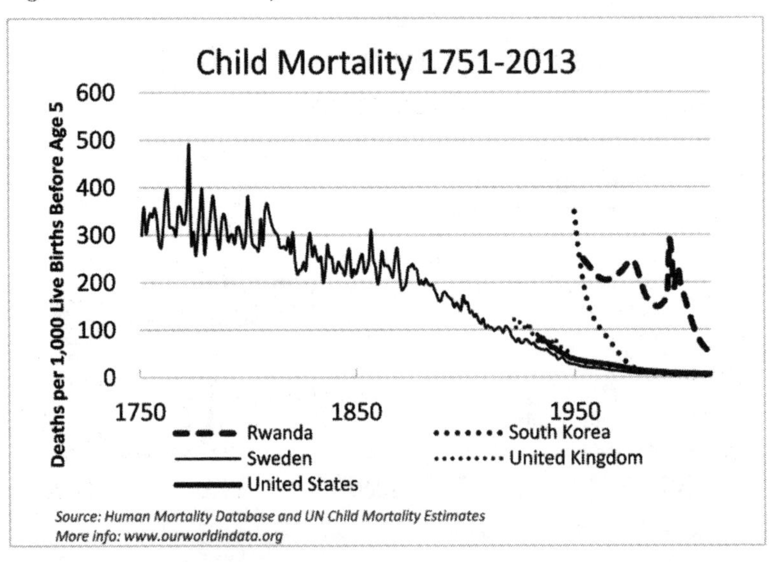

Figure 22 Child Mortality Rates

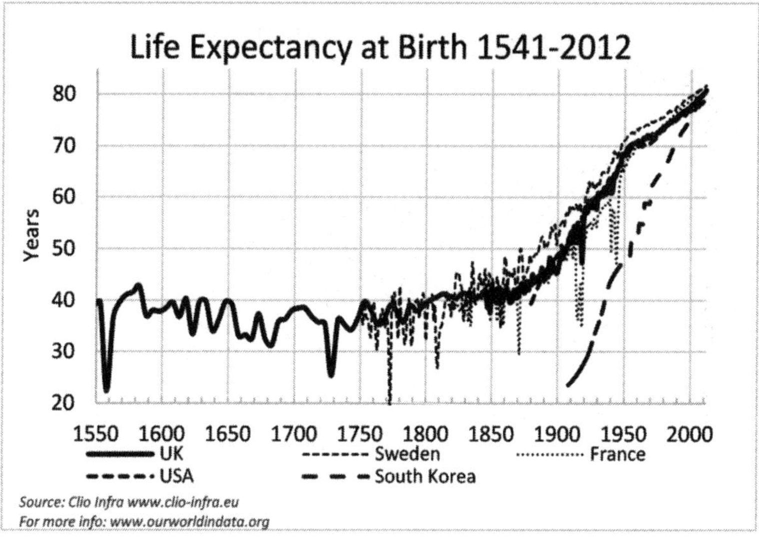

Figure 23 Life Expectancy

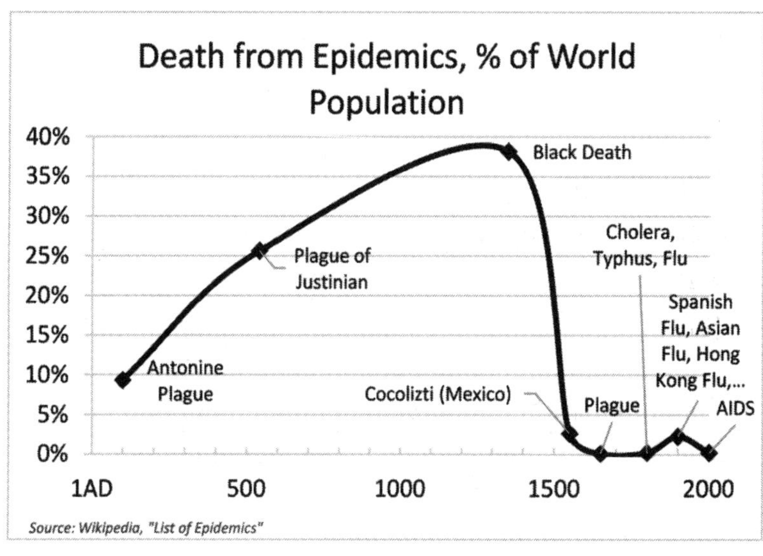

Figure 24 Death from Epidemics

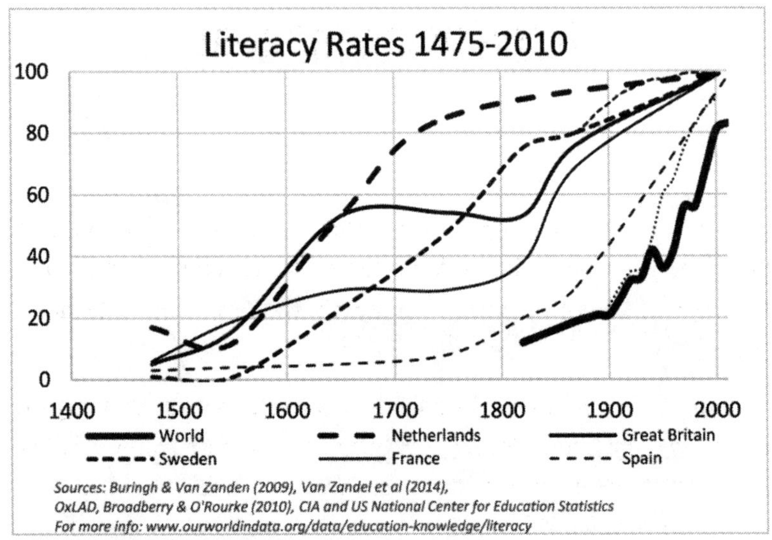

Figure 25 Literacy Rates

Introducing Influent

Influent is a community of people and an online resource with books, videos and podcasts dedicated to the vision put forth in this book: developing leadership, building success, and influencing society.

Influent is continually updated with fresh content spanning the topics we care about: leadership, business, entrepreneurialism, and innovation, career development, growing in Christ, walking out a practical Christian lifestyle in your career and business, and changing the planet!

Connect with us: www.influent.life

Visit www.influent.life to join our community, access our video library, podcasts and other content. You can also find us on Facebook, Twitter (/influentlife), and LinkedIn (Influent Life). Share your thoughts, contribute to future content, and connect with the author and thousands of others who are walking out their own path of leadership and influence.